What D
Say—Ho
Wen

What Did Jesus Really Say—How Christianity Went Astray

✦

[What To Say To A Born Again Christian Fundamentalist, But Never Had The Information]

Peter Cayce

iUniverse, Inc.
New York Lincoln Shanghai

What Did Jesus Really Say—How Christianity Went Astray

[What To Say To A Born Again Christian Fundamentalist, But Never Had The Information]

Copyright © 2005 by Peter Cayce

iUniverse books may be ordered through booksellers or by contacting:

iUniverse
2021 Pine Lake Road, Suite 100
Lincoln, NE 68512
www.iuniverse.com
1-800-Authors (1-800-288-4677)

ISBN: 0-595-32673-0

Printed in the United States of America

Dedicated

To

Jeshua

Contents

CHAPTER 1   I'm Not A Christian Anymore, But I Really Do Like Jesus 1

CHAPTER 2   The Influence Of Jesus (A Brief Transitional Chapter) 9

CHAPTER 3   A Brief History Of Christianity (Just Enough To Make A Point) 11

CHAPTER 4   Dating Jesus' Death And The Gospels (Which Gospel Is Most Reliable?) 18

CHAPTER 5   Problems With Translating The New Testament Gospels 21

CHAPTER 6   More Gospel Discrepancies And Problems 24

CHAPTER 7   The Problem With Paul And John (And President G.W. Bush) 30

CHAPTER 8   Eternal Life (No Dogma Please, And Hold The Mustard) 41

CHAPTER 9   Sex, Marriage, And Homosexuality 44

CHAPTER 10   The Old Testament As A Source (Cut Off The Hands Of "Them" Women) 48

CHAPTER 11   Biblical Prophecy Of The Messiah Fulfilled? 51

CHAPTER 12   Jesus, Buddhism, And Kabbalah (A Brief Comparison) 58

CHAPTER 13   Science, Disillusionment, And The Existence Of
            God 62

Epilogue: Astrophysics, Karma, And How Everything In The
    Universe May Actually Work 67

Selected Bibliography. 77

1

I'm Not A Christian Anymore, But I Really Do Like Jesus

When the question of *What Did Jesus Really Say* came up for me, way back in the 1980s, I couldn't find any one book that simply answered this question. I searched through many old manuscripts, researched numerous theology books, interviewed many religious individuals, discussed comprehensive issues with religion scholars, and spent substantial amounts of time listening to an endless assembly of ministers, church instructors, and religious programs. I even pursued my undergraduate and graduate level degrees with these subjects in mind. Because I've also done a great deal of research into Esoteric Studies, and since I have studied many aspects of Religion and Philosophy throughout my entire life, there are some who have called me a *Twenty-first Century Philosopher*. I humbly accept that title. I even accept that designation with a certain amount of quiet pride.

It was also many years ago that I started this book. I wrote most of it in the late 1980s and shelved it away. I didn't see much of a demand for a book that questioned the precepts of Christianity, but I still felt I had to write it. I actually felt compelled to write it. I finally completed this book because of the recent resurgence of interest in Christianity, and because the need for it is probably greater today than ever before. For research, I went through nearly two hundred sources and manuscripts. While many were useful, some were not. Others seemed impervious to anything but their own particular dogma.

Subsequently, *What Did Jesus Really Say, How Christianity Went Astray* is written for all those interested in knowing what Jesus may have actually said—between the lines, so to speak—and also as an aid in simplifying the basic message of the New Testament. It's also written for the religious seeker or the interested skeptic who is simply fed up with being told what to believe by church authorities. The subjects in this book are also covered in a simplified context and easy-to-read summary, rather than in any detailed scholarly depth. Detailed analysis is certainly conducted when appropriate, but writing an overly dry scholarly book would clearly defeat my purpose of writing a straightforward introduction and an open-minded overview for the individual layman, religious seeker, or interested skeptic. This book is also somewhat unique in that it never denigrates Jesus, even though it frequently criticizes the precepts of Christianity, especially those of Fundamentalist Christianity. The problem, therefore, is not with Jesus. The problem is with Christians, particularly Fundamentalist Christians, and with what they have done to the teachings of Jesus.

Furthermore, a good deal of pain and effort has been made to check, verify, and then reconfirm the various facts, statements, and other information in this book with reliable sources (whether the subject is religion or astrophysics or anything in between). I also have not allowed anything to remain that is subject to inaccuracy, imagination, or flimsy guesswork. In short, I've always been a writer who never liked quoting anything unless I knew it was accurate and true. I expect it of myself. I expect it of others. I even expect it of Christianity. Hence, you now know the primary reason for me writing this book. If it's not asking too much, I simply want to know the basic underlying truth of anything and everything that I'm interested in. This includes my interest in Christianity. For those of you who also wish to delve further and deeper into this subject, I have included a *Selected Bibliography*, at the end of this book, with approximately forty-five of the most relevant sources that specifically relate to the issues at hand.

That being said, various denominations of Christianity have their own specific doctrines and teachings. My goal, however, has been to keep Christianity as pure and uncomplicated as possible. In essence, Christianity should be based on the teachings of Jesus Christ and not on the teachings of the church over the last twenty centuries. Certainly many Christian denominations have prospered because people believed their leaders had found the "truth." I'm not saying that these churches shouldn't exist or prosper, but once again, for something to be called Christianity, the religion should logically follow the teachings of Jesus Christ—just as Buddhism, for example, should follow the teachings of The Buddha—otherwise why call it Christianity? Nevertheless, over the many years that I have researched and studied Christianity, I have developed a great respect for Jesus. I've often wished that I could go back in time and personally hear him teach. In many ways, I see Jesus as something of a unique role model for humanity. His example, however, often appears beyond human capacity to follow, and although I can't honestly say I'm a disciple of Jesus (which has far too many uncomfortable, dogmatic, and Christian Fundamentalist overtones for my liking), I do like to consider myself an admirer and supporter of his teachings.

Another catalyst for writing this book occurred in 1985. I had stumbled onto a weekly television program that usually prompted me to keep changing channels. It turned out to be a fervent and sweaty Jimmy Swaggert television sermon that I'd seen similar versions of before. This time the preacher's theme was on premarital sex and abortion with a little ultraconservative politics thrown in. I don't think I need to mention his point of view, but for those readers who might be just visiting Earth and thinking of applying for a "planetary visa or green card"—if there were such a thing—he was very much against these practices. Mr. Swaggert was passionately expressing some of the various conservative views of Christian Fundamentalists, a group that is sometimes known in some circles as the far right wing of the Republican Party. Swaggert was ultimately dislodged from his evangelical television role, in 1988, by a Christian Fundamentalist organization, *The Assemblies of God*, after a major scandal that associated him with prostitutes.

Jimmy Swaggert, however, was not the first dogmatic Christian that I'd ever heard or seen. I remember arguing with a church instructor, when I was just twelve years old, about whether Judas was suffering for eternity in Hell for betraying Jesus. What a scene that was. The church pastor actually had to intervene. I was ultimately told to just accept what the church knows to be true. This, consequently, became my first real life encounter with a Fundamentalist-like Christian who tried to force me to believe his religious point of view. When it comes to Christian indoctrination, however, this process of religious "brainwashing" is not that unusual. Like many children brought up in an evangelical church environment, I was inundated with an enormous amount of religious and dogmatic teaching. This sometimes amounts to a form of classical conditioning that any behavioral or Pavlovian psychologist could be proud of. While some of these children will forget the religious teachings as fast as they learn them, perhaps these are the lucky ones, others will wrestle with religious concepts and morality issues for many years. For this latter group, indoctrinated concepts will often rise to the surface for further investigation by the individual. By the nature of this book alone, if nothing else, I fall into this latter group. Many of you reading this will also fall into this group.

Over the last thirty years, I have also found that the one common denominator among evangelical preachers is that most adhere to a strict literal interpretation of the Bible. They believe that the Bible is the "true infallible Word of God." Because many Christians also believe that the original writing and translation of the Bible occurred under the controlling auspices and guidance of the Holy Spirit—and since God is perfect and since the Holy Spirit is God (being part of the Trinity aspect of God)—then it follows suit that the Bible should be flawless. We will examine this flawless issue in greater detail since the New Testament certainly has many minor flaws as well as some very major significant flaws.

For the most part, bible thumping evangelists (no disrespect intended) also firmly adhere to the King James Version of the Holy Bible, although this particular version is probably marred with the greatest amount of error. It should therefore be understood that the Bible is influenced by human error, and that truth itself, maybe even God's truth, could very well exist within its pages. Nevertheless, well-intentioned early churchmen have also elaborated on and changed the original message of Jesus Christ on whose teachings Christianity should logically be based. All these issues will be discussed later in this book.

A sincere and honest attempt also needs to be made in deciphering the accuracy of the Gospel translations—and the uniformity of the overall message—with the hopeful result of uncovering truth in its simplest form. By doing this, one can become increasingly absorbed with Jesus, the Bible, the concept of a Messiah, and Christianity as a whole. In addition, what Jesus actually said becomes far more important than listening to what well-meaning Christian churches have to say. This is especially true for Born Again Christians who often alienate non-Christians, and even other Christians, with a frequently inflexible, dogmatic, politically conservative, and morality-pushing form of Christianity. This is unfortunate since these Fundamentalist Christians are usually well-meaning folk whose underlying intention is to basically help others by trying to save them, or more specifically, to help others come to Jesus so that he can save them.

As for myself, I'd probably call myself a religious eclectic. I pursued my undergraduate and graduate level degrees in both Religion and Philosophy and conducted over 30 years of research into such religions and practices as Christianity, Mysticism, Indian and Chinese Buddhism, Kabbalah, Judaism, the lesser known Eckankarism, Mythology, Reincarnationism, Latin, and Greek. I also have a lifelong fascination and a deep abiding interest in the subjects of Astronomy and Astrophysics. In many ways, these two subjects add to the philosophical appreciation I have about the grandeur and magnificence of an approximately fifteen billion year old universe that contains billions of galaxies with hundreds of millions (and even hundreds of billions) of stars per galaxy.

I have also interviewed many Christians, had numerous discourses with Born Again ministers and evangelists, and spoken with many denominational groups such as Catholics, Presbyterians, Lutherans, Episcopalians, Baptists, and even

Jews for Jesus. As a writer and researcher, I've attended Adult Christian religion classes, had roaming Jehovah Witnesses in my home, collected various information from groups such as the Mormons, and listened to thousands of hours of religious teaching on television, radio, and in churches. I had even investigated psychics, spiritualists, and psychic phenomenon during the 1980's while conducting comprehensive research into Mysticism and Spiritualism.

Finally, I might even call myself a Jungian or Freudian except that I had a broader religious background than most, over and above what was just previously mentioned, which consisted of seven straight years of religious studies. This included daily weekday instruction in a Lutheran religious educational facility as well as affiliated evangelical studies each and every Saturday and Sunday. If this were not enough of a religious foundation, I also accumulated three years of Catholic Theology from both Jesuit priests and Salesian brothers. Consequently, with an intimate knowledge of Christianity at my disposal, I began to seriously ask, "…what are these Born Again Christian Fundamentalists talking about?" Although they may seem a bit outlandish at times, for the most part I believe them to be equally sincere in their beliefs. Nevertheless, biblical scripture—when given a strict and rigid interpretation—often becomes unbending dogma that drives a wedge between the fervent Born Again Christian Fundamentalist and those who are willing to listen, but not to closed-minded dogmatism.

Unbending dogma has also been used to condemn the morality of those who may support a particular ideology or way of life such as abortion, birth control, same sex relationships, premarital sex, gay marriages, and more. These differences also put the Christian Fundamentalist at political odds with those who disagree with them on these and other sensitive issues. This could even be part of the problem in the United States today. Modern day Christianity may be unwittingly helping to separate the U.S.A. into "two countries" with two more or less separate ideologies. Recent national polls tend to reinforce this argument (National Survey of Religion & Politics, University of Akron). For example, people who consider themselves religious and who regularly attend a church service are more likely to be conservative and vote Republican. Those who don't consider themselves to be overly religious and who don't regularly attend a church service are more likely to be liberal and vote Democrat (USA Today/CNN/Gallup Polls, May 2004). In some ways, the United States may be as divided today as it was in the 1800's when four decades of intense political, economic, and social differences split this country apart into two distinct and opposing ideologies that ultimately culminated in the American Civil War.

In any case, religion is not only a matter of ideology or faith, it must also be one of the mind. Blind faith is not the solution when the mind continually beckons for reasonable and legitimate answers. Yet for many Fundamentalist Christians, inner doubts and questions are sometimes repressed because that's what the faithful are expected to do. Sometimes these internal questions are even attributed to evil suggestions from Satan and should therefore be ignored. These mental doubts can also be attributed to "the sins of the flesh" that have been brought about by a sinful mind and by the first sin of Adam and Eve in the Garden of Eden. The mind, the emotions, and the spirit, however, can and must agree with each other. There should be whole agreement and understanding within an individual. If not, the religion can sometimes cause more harm than good, or it merely functions as morality with the added attribute of a deity. Many psychologists, such as Freud's protege Carl Jung, believed religion to be this type of deity inspired morality.

While this inner conflict continues, truth appears to become considerably elusive and confused. When the inner conflict eventually resolves itself, a self-righteous certainty of being correct may incorporate itself. Sometimes you will hear how overzealous newly converted Fundamentalist Christians have been "born again" and how their lives have been dramatically changed due to their faith and commitment to Jesus. I have no doubt that the lives of many Born Again Christians have been changed for the better. Thus their initial attempts to have you experience this same peace of mind can be a very admirable quality. Once again, it's even a little heartbreaking when you recognize that their initial intention is to genuinely help their fellow man, even if the help is sometimes unwanted.

It is also important to understand that not all Christians and evangelists are unbending fanatics, although dogmatic behavior, when it does exist, is usually reinforced by ministers, peers, reading the Bible, and other church oriented functions. If this were all there was to it, I would say that Christianity is just another religion. Let them be. No harm done. But this is not the case. Not only does Christianity have a violent and manipulative history—although this may or may not be relevant for our times—conservative Christians today are getting more and more involved in politics in an attempt to elect politicians who will change the laws that Christians find unacceptable. According to exit polls in the 2004 Bush vs. Kerry presidential election, one of five voters in the key swing state of Ohio was an evangelical Christian (NBC/MSNBC, 11/02/04). Of these particular Christian voters, 75% of them voted for Conservative/Republican George W. Bush.

As of 2004, our Supreme Court is also basically conservative in nature. Reagan appointed Rehnquist, O'Connor, Scalia, and Kennedy. George H. Bush appointed Souter and Thomas. Some of these Justices even seem ready for retirement, or worse, they could pass away while a conservative President is in office. The Clinton-appointed, non-conservative, Ruth Bader Ginsberg is in her 70s. Another more liberal Justice, John Paul Stevens, is in his 80s. The death of any human being can certainly be a tragic circumstance, but it's even worse when the direction of a country can be changed by such an event. After all, the Supreme Court helped influence the presidential election in the year 2000. One more conservative Justice appointed by a conservative President could also prompt the overthrow of the crucial Roe v. Wade case that made abortion legal. This could bring us back to the days when women were having unsafe and even dangerous abortions in the dirty, hidden, back offices of illegal abortion doctors. As unfortunate and regrettable as abortion is, the right to perform or have this type of medical procedure should not be made a criminal act.

Lastly, I lost a very old friend of nearly 28 years to Born Again Christian Fundamentalism. She ultimately cut me off because I often wanted to discuss issues related to the New Testament and Jesus. She felt that I was trying to undermine her beliefs. In some ways, I was questioning her beliefs, but my questions were never meant as an attack. All I wanted to do was have a logical discussion on religious ideas and theology. Unfortunately, Fundamentalist Christianity doesn't argue well when confronted with logic. Christians will ultimately tell you that "…you just have to have faith." For these reasons and others, becoming a Fundamentalist Christian is very much like joining a religious cult—although you will NEVER get a Fundamentalist Christian to admit this—and just as my old friend had done with me, personal ties are eventually severed to those non-Christians whom they feel they just cannot "save."

Once again, you should always remember that the Born Again Christian's underlying goal is to help you find Jesus and become saved. According to these Fundamentalists, believing in Jesus as the Son of God and as your personal savior is the only way to get to Heaven. All others go to Hell and suffer eternal damnation and torture. There are simply no other options. None. They maintain that you must put all doubt aside and fully believe that Jesus died for your sins, but did Jesus really say we needed to believe this about him? Actually, he does not. Jesus never stresses this issue in the New Testament Gospels of Matthew, Mark, and Luke. Other New Testament writers also do not make this claim. Only John and Paul make Jesus a prerequisite condition of whether we go to Heaven or Hell. As will be discussed later in this book, the written testimony of both Paul and John are very much subject to question. They are simply not reliable sources. At the very least, we must give them far less credence than Matthew, Mark, and Luke. Subsequently, if you remove Paul and John from the New Testament equation, the divinity and savior aspects of Jesus are no longer the focus of the New Testament. Instead, Jesus' message comes through, more or less, loud and clear. Since this "Jesus as Savior" issue is really of very great importance, and will sometimes cause various levels of concern and trepidation among those who are drifting away from Christianity, a more thorough evaluation of this specific doctrine will also be made. Once again, what Jesus <u>Christ</u> taught and what <u>Christian</u>ity teaches are often not the same thing.

Finally, this book is dedicated to all those people who have told me over the years (and I am paraphrasing) that they don't have a problem with Jesus, they just have "…a real problem with Christianity and with Christian morality." When some of these same people also found out that I was writing this book, I heard such comments as "…just give us some truth." Subsequently, with all due diligence, I will now undertake to give you that truth. The whole truth. And nothing but the truth. So help me God.

At the end of this book—within the Epilogue—a compelling theory is also proposed on how everything in the universe might actually work that touches on Jesus, God, Karma, Buddhism, Kabbalah, Reincarnation, Science, Physics, Astronomy, and even Astrophysics. And at the risk of sounding arrogant, which is certainly not my intention, here comes the simple truth. So help me God.

2

The Influence Of Jesus
(A Brief Transitional Chapter)

The influence of Jesus cannot be denied. Jesus (Yeshua in Aramaic, Yehoshua in Hebrew, Issa in Arabic, and Iesous in Greek) has received more fame and even notoriety, in some circles, than any other individual in history. In some respects, Jesus was mankind's misguided reason for countless murders during the Inquisition and Holy Wars. The early church also persecuted individuals in an attempt to repress scientific thought, particularly Alchemy (Chemistry), because it all too closely resembled what the church considered magic. The persecution of Galileo is only another example of religious fanaticism at its worst. Joan of Arc being burned alive at the stake is no less tragic.

On a more positive note, Jesus has been the spark for missionary work that feeds the hungry in all parts of the world. Perhaps more so than any other individual in human history, Jesus has been mankind's inspiration for numerous humanitarian efforts at alleviating human suffering. These include such endeavors that provide medical, financial, and agricultural assistance to poverty stricken nations.

Jesus has also "graced" the cover of *Time* and *Newsweek* magazines. He has been the focus of numerous dramatic plays, movies, and artistic renditions throughout the last 2,000 years. Most notably and most recently, Mel Gibson's multimillion dollar worldwide box office hit, *The Passion of Christ,* has brought a great deal of attention to the subject of Christianity and Jesus. Other dramatic musicals and popular portrayals are *Jesus Christ Superstar* and *Godspell,* which were also converted into film. Franco Zeffirelli's critically acclaimed movie *Jesus of Nazareth* is another example. *The Greatest Story Ever Told* is yet another film rendition of Jesus. Painters have also been inspired by Jesus and have created countless numbers of paintings during the Renaissance and other historical ages (i.e., Leonardo da Vinci, Botticelli, Caravaggio, Michelangelo, etc.).

Although the influence of Jesus is certainly not in question, some have questioned whether Jesus actually existed at all, but there are many comprehensive non-biblical records that verify the existence of Jesus. A major compilation of these works was published in Cambridge, in 1923, by C.R. Haines, entitled *Heathen Contact With Christianity During Its First Century And A Half.*

The comprehensive records of Josephus, who lived from A.D. 37 to approximately A.D. 100, are also extremely insightful since Josephus provides eyewitness testimony related to the growth and development of first century Christianity and Western Civilization in general. Josephus had also been a member of the Jewish priestly aristocracy and was ultimately taken prisoner during the Jewish revolt against Rome (A.D. 66 to A.D. 70). Josephus eventually became an advisor and historian to the Roman Empire and served three Roman Emperors: (1) Vespasian, (2) Titus, and (3) Domitian. The records of Josephus' are extremely valuable because his reports are very matter of fact and neutral in nature. He's a straightforward historian who appears dedicated to accurately reporting the historical facts. His non-biased records are also important since they're the earliest references to Jesus outside of the New Testament.

Other extensive records of Jesus are contained in the Gnostic *Nag Hammadi Library* published in 1977. These Gnostic texts will also be briefly discussed later in this book. In any case, it is clear that Jesus was more than a fleeting *"Jesus Christ Superstar,"* but before we can start an overall analysis related to the important question of *What Did Jesus Really Say,* we need to take a brief look at the overall history of Christianity to see *How Christianity Went Astray.*

3

A Brief History Of Christianity (Just Enough To Make A Point)

The Roman Empire tolerated many religions and religious cults as long as they were loyal to the Roman Empire. Christianity, although illegal in the first two centuries, was not initially considered a serious enough threat for Rome to try and wipe out the practice. For example, the Jews were more or less accepted as long as they were loyal to the Roman Emperor. The Jews were always a difficult people to rule, but Rome only became determined to stamp out their Jewish "problem" in A.D. 66 when the Jews began a violent revolt. Roman forces ultimately burned Jerusalem to the ground in A.D. 70, and in the process of fighting this rebellion, the forces of the Roman Empire also demolished many written records, documents, and texts. This more than likely included New Testament records written in the language of Jesus. To this day, we still have no original Aramaic manuscripts from the archaeological era of first century Palestine. All we have are the secondary sources: the Greek translations.

Nevertheless, Christians were certainly victimized and oppressed during the first century, but they only became seriously persecuted and despised by the Roman Empire during the second and third centuries. According to Roman historian Tactitus, Emperor Nero blamed the Christians for the catastrophic fire that nearly destroyed Rome in A.D. 64. Before this event, Romans simply thought of Christians—if they knew of them at all—as one of the many obscure cults that were tolerated by the Roman Empire. By the second century, however, many rumors and misconceptions about Christianity had developed. The Eucharist was misinterpreted as a form of cannibalism since Christians were eating the "body" and drinking the "blood" of Christ. This was an extremely bizarre concept for Romans. Christians were also considered immoral and involved in incest and orgies as "brothers and sisters in Christ." They were even thought to be involved in worshiping the genitals of their priests. For some Romans, Christians were also believed to be involved in human sacrifice and infanticide as well as drinking the blood of children who had been sacrificed (Minutius Felix, in his dialogue *Octavius*, approximately A.D. 170). Some of these beliefs also basically originated from second century rumors of a Christian cult and the human sacrifice of the cult-god's son, Jesus. For the Romans, everything they heard about Christianity seemed to revolve around some kind of religious human sacrifice.

Early Christians were not only oppressed by the Romans, however, they were also repressed by other Christians. As early as the first century, Gentile Christians were developing a reputation for suppressing their Jewish counterparts. Christian writings, written by Jews, were frowned upon and ignored. Fragmented and semi-fragmented copies of some of these early Christian writings, written in Coptic, were only discovered in 1945, in Nag Hammadi, Egypt. All other Aramaic records had either been destroyed or are still hidden away somewhere. In fact, these first century documents would have been destroyed by Jewish authorities (who would have clearly wanted these texts eliminated), but they may also have been destroyed by early Gentile Christians who were trying to separate themselves from Jewish traditions and customs. As one can see, the first century was an extremely turbulent era. Between the Romans, the Jews, and even Gentile Christians, it's not too surprising that we have absolutely no original, first century, Aramaic texts about Jesus.

In any case, it was not until the year A.D. 311 that the Roman Emperor Constantine, the first Christian Emperor, essentially made Christianity legal alongside many other existing pagan practices and religious cults. For the first time in almost 2½ centuries, Christians could finally worship in public without legal repercussions, persecutions, and ramifications from the Roman Empire. Constantine also asked the bishops of every country to come to Nicaea in the year A.D. 325. This gathering was known as the First Council of Nicaea and brought as many as 150 to 300 bishops together (the exact figure is not known; some records suggest a figure as high as 2,000). Nevertheless, Nicaea was ideally situated. This city made it geographically feasible for bishops to come from most of the provinces of the Roman Empire. Bishops arrived from Asia, Greece, Thrace, Syria, Palestine, and Egypt. Some even traveled from outside of the Roman Empire, from as far away as Persia.

Emperor Constantine is therefore credited for bringing many church leaders together at Nicaea and also at Nova Roma (later called Constantinople) to work out the various differences early Christians had. These questions included the divinity of Jesus and the concept of a Trinity (God the Father, Son, and Holy Spirit). They also debated on what writings would ultimately be included in the church approved canon of the New Testament Bible. The Gospel of Thomas, which is considered to be one of the most authoritative with sayings specifically attributed to Jesus, was ignored and eliminated. The Gospel of Mary Magdalene, the Gospel of James the Just, The Gospel of Philip, and many other texts about Jesus were also omitted. This comprehensive deletion of texts—associated with Jewish people who knew Jesus and who had heard him speak—always seems regrettable. It's almost as if the New Testament has something lacking. These missing books should have been included to provide a more comprehensive view of Jesus and to further clarify what he may have actually said. In any case, Christianity ultimately becomes a state religion in A.D. 379, becomes the majority religion of the Roman Empire by the next century, and ultimately gains more and more power during this time.

By the early Middle Ages, with the election of Pope Gregory the Great in A.D. 590, attempts were made to turn the remaining barbarians of Europe into allies since they still posed a threat to Christianity. Pope Gregory the Great—the son of a Roman senator and grandson of Pope Felix III—established monasteries and missionaries during this time. He instructed such monks as Saint Augustine of Canterbury to destroy as few pagan temples as possible and to accept as many pagan practices as necessary, but only those that were more or less compatible with Christianity. The Pope's thinking was to integrate the non-Christian barbarians of Europe with Christianity. This was a commendable time for Christianity. It seemed to be valiantly trying to find a compromise to differing belief structures.

Pope Gregory the Great, however, is also generally credited for turning Mary Magdalene into a prostitute. Women were beginning to gain power and authority in the early church, and Mary Magdalene seemed to represent female strength and authority to many at the time. After all, the Apostle Paul had clearly stated,"**…Let your women keep silent in the churches, for they are not permitted to speak…and if they want to learn something, let them ask their own husbands at home…**" **(1 Corinthians 14:34-35, NKJV).** Since there is absolutely no discussion in the New Testament Gospels about Mary Magdalene ever being a prostitute, turning Mary Magdalene into a "whore" was an effective way of discouraging women's growing role in the early church. Nevertheless, the Gospels do state that Mary was very close to Jesus and that he had a special relationship with her. In fact, according to the New Testament, Mary is honored by being the first to see Jesus after he had resurrected from the dead. Not only did Pope Gregory have some trouble with this, but Jesus' disciples also didn't understand. The disciples don't even believe Mary when she excitedly tells them that she has seen the risen Jesus. Their bottom line question seemed to be, if Jesus had really resurrected from the dead, why should Mary Magdalene be chosen to see him first? Why wouldn't one of Jesus' very own "hand-picked" disciples see him first? Jesus certainly cared deeply for Mary. She is clearly a devoted follower of Jesus. But why Mary? Recent books such as *The DaVinci Code* and the movie *The Last Temptation of Christ*, which both theorize that Jesus may have married Mary Magdalene, have no biblical basis. They are pure speculative fiction, but neither the author nor the filmmaker really make a claim that their work is factual. In any case, with the apparent help of Pope Gregory the Great, Mary Magdalene becomes a prostitute for the first time nearly 600 years after her death, and her position of authority in the church is also diminished with her newly appointed designation and classification as a harlot.

Five hundred years later in A.D. 1095, Christianity takes a significant turn for the worse. Pope Urban II made the spread of Christianity much more forceful. No longer were attempts made to peacefully integrate non-Christians with Christians. Pope Urban II called for an armed holy war known as the Holy Crusades. This was a very violent and bloody time for Christianity. In A.D. 1099, these Crusaders captured Jerusalem and placed a Christian king on its throne. They then went to war against other non-Christians, mostly Muslims, all in the name of Jesus Christ, on such issues as forcing others to become baptized. Although political power and the conquest of lands may also have been underlying or even "subconscious" motivations, the primary mission of these Holy Crusaders was to convert others to Christianity—because this is what God wanted them to do.

Nevertheless, after eight violent holy wars, these Crusaders were only successful in Europe and along the Northwest Mediterranean (i.e., the Kingdom of Jerusalem, the County of Tripoli, the Principality of Antioch, and the County of Edessa). The Muslims had resisted these Christian warriors and fought back hard. They eventually recaptured Jerusalem. Christian Crusades against Syria were also defeated. Ultimately we see the remnants of these Holy Crusades today. The Muslim world currently dominates the Middle East, and Christianity dominates Europe.

During the times of these Crusades, monasteries were also becoming major money generating enterprises. Since monks were considered more pious than other ordinary members of medieval society, they were considered to have a much better "link to God." Since the prayers of pious men were also thought to be more readily heard by God, many wealthy people began to make use of this great spiritual resource. It was also thought that soldiers might have a tougher time getting into Heaven. At one point, the church required 120 days of penance for every person that a Holy Crusader killed in battle. Subsequently, if a warrior were to kill 1,000 men in battle, penance could take 120,000 days (nearly 329 years) before receiving absolution from the church. Since an individual could never do this on his own, especially if the death toll was considerably higher, it was believed that monks could help with the process. Monks were subsequently "paid" to help conduct these prayers. A king could even employ hundreds of monks in many monasteries to pray for him. For example, the monastery in Glastonbury, England, actually became quite successful and affluent by providing this type of penance oriented service.

In a bizarre and unexpected twist, Pope Urban II significantly reduced the practice of monks doing penance for those who had killed others in battle. The Pope simply changed the policy that required penance for killing. He basically proclaimed that it was acceptable to kill another individual as long as that person was not a Christian. Killing Muslims, therefore, became an acceptable practice in the eleventh century. Killing in the name of Jesus Christ and Christianity, in some peculiar form of rationalization, actually became the penance itself. Monks certainly continued to provide this type of service for an appropriate financial donation, but the demand for requiring enormous amounts of penance for killing a non-Christian was no longer needed. Nevertheless, there was still enough "sin" being committed so that monks continued to take on the act of penance for others when the proper financial stipend was provided. Prayer, therefore, was still a highly valuable commodity for these eleventh century monks.

A great deal of the money that came into these monasteries was also placed into medieval "real estate" and in building enormous cathedrals. A monastery would even build and organize the town that surrounded it. If someone stood at the top of a monastery's lofty cathedral or its bell tower, one could often see all the land and buildings that it owned for as far as the eye could see. Whole towns were often under the jurisdiction of a particular monastery, sometimes to the financial frustration and disadvantage of many of its townspeople. Monasteries basically took a percentage of everyone's business revenue. They even collected a percentage of horse droppings and cow manure since these defecations had monetary value as fertilizer. In other words, any business that operated within the monastery's jurisdiction provided revenue. Monks even issued summonses and fines as well as collected revenues from these infractions.

Other monks, such as the Cistercians, attempted to break away from the status quo and follow a path that reflected a true vow of poverty, but as long as prayer was considered a financial commodity, and as long as people were willing to pay for penance, Christianity would always be treading on dangerous ground.

Even the Cistercians eventually succumbed to the temptation of financial materialism. Unfortunately, the best laid plans and intentions of Christianity have always succumbed to the lure of monetary enticement. The ultimate result is that money eventually corrupts spirituality. Research even shows that some bishops were financially operating and managing brothels. It was also not uncommon for monks to regularly frequent these facilities. In A.D. 1358, the Grand Council of Venice even declared that prostitution was necessary for the world of the Middle Ages to function properly (Richards 1994). Regardless of the sin being committed, as long as people were in need of forgiveness for their vices, the church was always there to provide the necessary amnesty and clemency and to collect the appropriate donation for doing so.

During the Spanish Inquisition (1478–1834), records also show that many people were tortured for being so-called heretics. If someone was a repeat offender—and for those who would not repent their heresies—being burned at the stake was frequently the outcome. People also languished in prison for questioning things in the Bible. A simple question of whether Jesus was the Son of God, or whether the mother of Jesus was a virgin, could prompt anyone to contact the religious authorities. Members of the Inquisition could then begin an investigation. The accuser could even remain anonymous. What someone was accused of could also be kept secret; this itself was against the laws of Spain, but it was done nonetheless. Those who were questioned and detained were initially Jews, then Moors, and then Lutherans. Eventually ordinary Christians were questioned based on their behavior. Those who rejected or criticized the Inquisition were also viewed as rejecting God.

During the papacy reign of Pope Sixtus IV (1471–1484), the Inquisition implemented methods of torture that included forcing a long towel or rag down a heretic's throat. When it could not be forced any further, water was poured onto the rag. This would saturate the material and prompt uncontrolled swallowing until the towel reached the stomach. At that point, the cloth would be pulled out with excruciating pain to the victim involved.

In A.D. 1492, Spain's Queen Isabella (the same monarch who commissioned Christopher Columbus) had also given the Jews that were living in Spain an ultimatum. They either had to convert to Christianity or they had to leave the country. Spies became quite common. People turned others into the authorities. Treachery became synonymous with the politics of Christianity, and everything, of course, was basically done in the misguided name of Jesus Christ.

By the time of the Protestant Reformation in the 1500's, many aspects of the Christian Church and the papacy had become corrupt. The expression, power is corrupting, is a term that aptly describes Christianity at that time. The church even sold *indulgences* so that Christians could buy their way out of their sins. For the right price, you could even bypass Purgatory and get to heaven before your neighbor. In 1521, Martin Luther, a Catholic monk, became fed up with this corruption and became the first rebellious reformer to break away from the Catholic Church. This "protest" resulted in Lutheranism and ultimately marked the beginning of the Protestant Reformation.

Several centuries later, in 1808, Napoleon and his French forces ended the Inquisition when they conquered Spain. When France was invaded, and after Napoleon was sent into exile in 1814, the Inquisition was able to once again obtain a political foothold—and just like a cancer that is hard to eliminate—the Inquisition made something of a comeback by 1818. The Inquisition was finally abolished sixteen years later in 1834.

Subsequently, from all of the preceding history, I am now reminded of one of Jesus' statements about how **"…a tree is known by its fruit" (Matthew 12:33, NKJV)** (also Matthew 7:16-20). If one looks at a prophet or a religion, as Jesus suggests, and sees what results it puts forth, one can ultimately see the "fruit" that it produces. In other words, if Jesus' words are accurate and appropriate, then hasn't Christianity frequently produced a significant amount of bad fruit?

In any case, that's enough of a brief introductory history about Christianity. There's certainly a lot more we can talk about, including such subjects as the great witch hunts in Salem, Massachusetts or other more recent church corruption related to priests and the sexual abuse of children, but let's get back to a more important subject. The subject of Jesus Christ, and what **he** had to say.

4

Dating Jesus' Death And The Gospels
(Which Gospel Is Most Reliable?)

Although we can certainly acknowledge that Christianity hasn't had an overly positive or exemplary history, we still need to put Jesus into proper historical perspective. We will therefore use various non-secular sources such as Josephus, as well as biblical text, to ascertain the birth and death of Jesus. These records describe such events as the birth of Cleopatra, Julius Caesar, and Caesar Augustus (and how they chronologically relate to the life of Jesus). Many of these sources subsequently point to Jesus being born between 4 B.C. and A.D. 1, with his death occurring between A.D. 29 and A.D. 32.

According to New Testament Scripture, Jesus died on the eve of the Passover—just before the Sabbath on a Friday afternoon—and was resurrected on the third day. Some theorists dispute this. It's been suggested that Jesus was crucified on a Thursday, prior to a Friday High Passover, since his burial from Friday afternoon to Sunday morning would only constitute two days and nights (rather than the three days that the New Testament Gospels seem to indicate). According to calendar records, the Passover fell on a Saturday twice during that era. It first occurred on April 8, A.D. 30, and again on April 4, A.D. 33. The crucifixion of Jesus seems to have therefore occurred on April 7, A.D. 30. This cannot be construed as absolute fact, but in any event it appears that a gap of approximately forty years exists between the death of Jesus and the first written Greek Gospel translation.

Although various theories exist regarding the first Greek translation, scholars basically agree that Mark was probably written in the year A.D. 70, the translations of Matthew and Luke occurred between the years A.D. 80 and A.D. 90, and John was written between the years A.D. 90 and A.D. 100. Others similarly place the translation of Mark between the years A.D. 63 and A.D. 70, Matthew in approximately A.D. 70, Luke in the year A.D. 70 or A.D. 80, and John sometime around A.D. 90. The dating of these books has been considerably aided by the discovery of the lost *Dead Sea Scrolls* uncovered by archaeologists in this century. The records of these *Dead Sea Scrolls* include the first century Palestinian era of Jesus and have provided valuable information and insight into various aspects of the New Testament. It's also been ascertained that Matthew was probably written by a Jewish Christian for the Jews, while the books of Mark, Luke, and John are all written for non-Jewish Gentiles.

In addition, it has been theorized that an original Aramaic Matthew existed—written in approximately A.D. 40 to A.D. 49—which was an original source for the Greek translation of Matthew's Gospel. It is believed that this Aramaic text was lost along with any and all other manuscripts in the native language of Jesus. This seems corroborated by Christian Philosophers such as St. Irenaeus (late second century, the Bishop of Lyon, and considered the Founder of Christian Theology) and Origen (early third century and tortured for his Christian beliefs by the Romans). In their writings, they both state that the original Gospel of Matthew was written in the native Aramaic language of first century Palestine.

This is also substantiated by the fact that many Jews were expecting a Messiah during the Roman domination of first century Israel. Since Matthew was directed toward the Jews to prove through Old Testament prophecies that Jesus fulfilled these ancient prophecies, Matthew needed to be disseminated in Aramaic, the language of the first century Jewish people. This also seems confirmed by the fact that Matthew's Greek translation reflects a vocabulary that is Aramaic in nature. This is similar in analogy to the way we observe a language's idiomatic and grammatical syntaxes. It is also somewhat analogous to how we can distinguish Shakespearean English from modern English, or how we might notice the way Italians verbalize the English language vs. how the Chinese might use it (i.e., verb/noun placement, subject/predicate usage, position of adjectives or pronouns, etc.).

Matthew may also have been translated from a lost original source, probably Aramaic, which has been called "Q" (abbreviated from the German term Quelle, which means source). If this theory is correct, then the Greek Matthew may be the most accurate of all the Gospels, primarily because translation may have occurred from a written source dated as early as ten years or less after Jesus' death, rather than forty to sixty years later. In other words, this is less time for the story of Jesus to be changed. It's therefore possible that Matthew may be a more reliable translation and a closer rendition to the actual teachings of Jesus. With further regard to ascertaining accuracy and reliability, Mark should also be given close scrutiny because it appears to be the very first New Testament translation in Greek.

Let's now take a brief look at any problems associated with translating the New Testament. We should certainly have valid concerns about whether the words of Jesus were accurately recorded and whether the Gospels and subsequent books of the Bible are a valid source of information.

5

Problems With Translating The New Testament Gospels

There is obvious wisdom in many of the parables, quotes, and sayings of the biblical Jesus. His presence in the Roman, Greek, and Hebrew world caused more than a fervor, and the influence of his life still touches hundreds of millions of people today. Nevertheless, because so many individuals believe that the Bible is 100% literal fact, it is important that Jesus' biblical words be put into clear understanding by logically looking at the translations and at the means of translation in order to avoid manipulation and interpretive error.

There are over five thousand Greek and eight thousand Latin manuscripts that support the New Testament. Although there are many variations, most correspond fairly closely. For quotations of Jesus, I basically used *The New King James Bible*. This also lists all of Jesus' quotes in red ink. I was hesitant, however, on using any Bible with the name "King James" inscribed on it even with the prefix "New":

> **"The King James Version of the New Testament was based upon a Greek text that was marred by mistakes, containing the accumulated errors of fourteen centuries of manuscript copying" (RSV Bible, p.vi).**

> **Whereas, "...the King James followed one of the versions, but where information is now available to resolve the problems, the New King James Version follows the Hebrew text" (NKJV, p.v).**

Regardless of the version, one drawback postulated by critics and biblical researchers is that the books of the New Testament are not the originals. The New Testament narratives had been passed down for some time by word of mouth. This presents the possibility of oral tradition errors. To use an analogy, if you line up fifty people and pass down a message from one individual to the next, the story has often changed by the time it reaches the last person. Sometimes considerably. The oral tradition was something of a sacred task for many, however, and as there were others who would know if the original story had changed, the Gospels were basically continued with little variation. In other words, the difference between an oral tradition and a written Christian text is not very significant when the oral tradition has become standardized by frequent repetition. Since there were also people in charge of preserving some of these oral traditions, very few significant changes were made to these biblical core stories (Dalpadado 1981).

The Synoptic texts of Matthew, Mark, and Luke clearly show this uniformity in story content. In short, Matthew, Mark, and Luke are far more reliable sources than the Gospel of John since all three basically tell the same story about Jesus. It is their uniformity in story content that truly gives them greater credence. The fact that John tells a different story about Jesus will also be discussed in greater detail in Chapter 7. In any case, the Gospels were reproduced by hand, over and over, with the accumulated errors of fourteen centuries of manuscript copying. With the invention of mechanical printing, all these accumulated errors culminated in a mechanically printed version produced in the year A.D. 1450. This version was then finalized in A.D. 1611 with the *Authorized Version* (then popularly known as the King James Bible; now known as the *King James Version*).

There are also several main problems with translating first century Palestinian Aramaic into Greek. First of all, there is an absence of vowel signs. The Aramaic word *di* is also a large problem. It functions as a conjunction that introduces object clauses and final clauses. It is used as a relative pronoun and can be either masculine, feminine, or neuter. It may include a demonstrative antecedent. It can be used to reflect possession. *Di* can also function as a conjunction that may introduce final clauses and object clauses.

Prepositional phrases can also be a problem. An example is found in Mark 4:4 (also Matthew 13:4 and Luke 8:5), **"...And it happened, as he sowed, that some seed fell by the wayside..." (NKJV).** The translation may actually be "...some seed fell **on** the road." The Aramaic prepositional phrase has more than one meaning, one of which being "besides the road" and another being "on the road." Seed that fell by the wayside (alongside the road) might logically be considered to germinate and grow, whereas seed would not be likely to grow **on** a road that was traveled by man, horses, and caravans. Since the whole point of the Mark 4 parable is that poorly distributed seed would not put forth roots, the phrase "on the road" would be a more logical translation. At any rate, this does not really change the meaning of the parable, but it does show that New Testament translations are prone to human error.

Another minor ambiguity is located in Mark 10:12 (also Luke 16:18), **"And if a woman divorces her husband and marries another, she commits adultery" (NKJV).** The translation might actually be, "And if a woman is divorced from her husband and marries another, she commits adultery." It's possible that the Greek translator misunderstood the participle verb to be in the active tense (divorcing her husband), but the Aramaic can also be translated in the passive (being divorced from her husband). According to Jewish historian, Josephus, this issue of divorce is corroborated by the fact that first century Jewish laws wouldn't allow a woman to divorce her husband. Once again, the Greek translations are prone to human error.

There are approximately one hundred of these ambiguities, but nothing very serious. It is nonetheless clear that the translation process was not perfect, even with the Holy Spirit overseeing the project.

6

More Gospel Discrepancies And Problems

Many minor discrepancies exist in the New Testament. Sometimes these discrepancies are minor. Other times they are very distinct and dramatic. For example, in Mark 6:8, Jesus commands the disciples to take nothing for their journey **"...except a staff."** In both Matthew 10:10 and Luke 9:3, the same basic story is told except the disciples are instructed to take nothing with them including **"...no staff."** This is certainly not a very dramatic variation, and the New Testament has many examples of this type. While these discrepancies do not detract from the overall message of Jesus' words, they do show that story variations and translation errors can occur. The New Testament stories simply have various differences.

Additional discrepancies include the fact that the biblical Jesus preaches the Beatitudes on a mountain in Matthew, **"Blessed are the poor...Blessed are the meek, for they shall inherit the earth" (Matthew 5:1-12, NKJV)**, but he preaches the Beatitudes on a level plain in Luke (Luke 6:17-23).

Jesus also first teaches the Lord's Prayer in Galilee, **"Our Father in heaven, hallowed be Your name" (Matthew 6:7-15, NKJV)**, but he teaches this prayer for the first time while on a road to Jerusalem in Luke (Luke 11:1-4).

Another larger ambiguity occurs in John 19:14. Here Jesus stands before Pilate in the sixth hour (12 Noon) before being crucified. In Mark 15:25, Jesus is crucified in the third hour (9 A.M.). It seems that this event, in particular, should have been recalled and recorded more accurately. It is certainly a critical key occurrence in the life of Jesus and with early Christians.

Larger and more serious problems exist in the New Testament. For example, there is a significant change in story content regarding Judas and his betrayal of Jesus (Matthew 27:3-7 and Acts 1:15-18). We have similar characters and situations in Matthew and Acts, but the stories are very different. In the account of

24

Matthew, Judas tries to return the 30 pieces of silver he received for betraying Jesus. He ultimately throws the coins into the temple when the chief priests refuse to accept the returned money. The chief priests, in turn, consider the coins "blood money" and purchase a piece of land (a potters field) to bury strangers in. Judas also hangs himself in remorse for betraying Jesus.

In the Book of Acts, we are told instead that Judas buys a piece of land with the "blood money." As punishment, God has Judas collapse to the ground and causes his body to violently burst open with all of his intestines (bodily entrails) gushing out. In other words, Judas does not hang himself at all. God kills him instead.

Which version is true? Is the author of Matthew or The Acts lying? Probably not. The story of Judas simply evolved and changed as it was passed from one individual to the next, but long periods of elapsed time, as in the Gospel of John, are not the cause for this particular distortion. The books of Matthew and The Acts were written during the same historical time period, in approximately A.D. 70 to A.D. 80. Whatever the reason for this major discrepancy, it should be apparent that we cannot take everything in the New Testament as 100% fact.

Another clear-cut, vivid, and major discrepancy occurs with the genealogy and lineage of Jesus (Luke 3:23-38/Matthew 1:1-17, NKJV). The difference is obvious:

LUKE	MATTHEW
1) Abraham	Abraham
2) Isaac	Isaac
3) Jacob	Jacob
4) Judah	Judah
5) Peroz	Peroz
6) Hezron	Hezron
7) Ram	Ram
8) Amminadab	Amminadab
9) Nahshon	Nahshon
10) Salmon	Salmon
11) Boaz	Boaz
12) Obed	Obed

LUKE	MATTHEW
13) Jesse	Jesse
14) King David	King David
15) Nathan	Solomon
16) Mattathah	Rehoboan
17) Menar	Abijah
18) Melea	Asa
19) Eliakim	Jehoshaphat
20) Jonan	Joram
21) Joseph	Uzziah
22) Judah	Jotham
23) Simeon	Ahaz
24) Levi	Hezekiah
25) Matthat	Manasseh
26) Jorim	Amon
27) Eliezer	Josiah
28) Jose	Jeconiah
29) Er	*SHEALTIEL
30) Elmodam	*ZERUBBABEL
31) Cosam	Abiud
32) Addi	Eliakim
33) Melchi	Azor
34) Neri	Zadok
35) *SHEALTIEL	Achim
36) *ZERUBBABEL	Eliud
37) Rhesa	Eleaza
38) Joannas	Matthan
39) Judah	Jacob

LUKE	MATTHEW
40) Joseph	*JOSEPH
41) Semei	*JESUS
42) Mattathiah	
43) Maath	
44) Naggai	
45) Esli	
46) Nahum	
47) Amos	
48) Mattathiah	
49) Joseph	
50) Janna	
51) Melchi	
52) Levi	
53) Matthat	
54) Heli	
55) *JOSEPH	
56) *JESUS	

Except for four corresponding names after King David, we have two different lists with two separate genealogies of Jesus. Not only this, we have fifteen extra names on Luke's list. Bearing this in mind, if each man had a son at the exact age of twenty—although the average age may be higher—approximately twenty years later his son might also have a son (assuming that each firstborn is a male). Since each new male generation would occur every twenty years or so, then it logically follows suit that 15 extra males x 20 years a generation (minimum) would produce a time discrepancy of at least 300 years or more.

In Josh McDowell's book, *Evidence That Demands A Verdict*, Mr. McDowell presents a possible explanation. He states that the genealogy listed in Matthew is that of Joseph and the one in Luke is that of Mary. He also states that Joseph did not father Jesus—the Holy Spirit had impregnated the Virgin Mary—so two separate genealogies were listed. A lineage for Mary and another lineage for Joseph were both provided to "cover all the bases" and to clearly show that Jesus was a descendant of ancient Israel's King David (1000 B.C. to 961 B.C.). Since the Old Testament prophecies state that the Messiah would be a descendant of King David, the writers of Matthew and Luke simply wanted to show that Jesus fulfilled this prophecy. Regardless of which lineage is used, they both trace back to King David

Mr. McDowell fails to answer the obvious. Why would Matthew depict Jesus as being conceived by the Holy Spirit (Matthew 1:18-20), yet still list the family blood line of Joseph. This is clearly a contradiction of logic. McDowell's explanation also doesn't explain the 300 minimum year variation in the genealogy. It's therefore not clear whether Matthew's genealogy is accurate or whether the information is correctly listed in Luke.

Another discrepancy occurs in Luke during the betrayal and arrest of Jesus in the Garden of Gethsemane (Matthew 26:51-56/Mark 14:47-52/Luke 22:51-53/John 18:10). As Jesus is being arrested, one of his followers draws a sword and cuts off the ear of Malchus, the chief priest's servant. Jesus heals Malchus' ear in Luke, but he does not do so in Matthew, Mark, or even in John. Remember that Matthew and Mark should be given first consideration in ascertaining what is accurate and reliable information. Logic would also dictate that if Jesus had really healed the servant's ear, those arresting him might have been hesitant in taking him away. Being an actual witness to an extraordinary miracle would have probably put the "fear of God" in their hearts. It's therefore possible that Luke may have elaborated on this story, or perhaps Matthew, Mark, and even John simply forgot to include this rather impressive miraculous event.

Furthermore, if Jesus' intention had been to be arrested—which apparently it was—would he have instigated such a dramatic walk-on-water type of miracle that might have prevented his arrest? Whether Jesus had really performed this miracle is not the issue. The simple fact is that the Gospels do not always tell the same stories. There are discrepancies.

Although there are many others, I'll list only one more example of ambiguity. It concerns the coming Kingdom of God and the awaited physical resurrection of the body into Heaven (Matthew 16:27-28/Mark 9:1/Mark 13:24-31/Luke 21:31-32/Luke 9:27/2 Thessalonians 2:1-7):

> **Jesus said "Assuredly, I say to you, there are some standing here who shall not taste death till they see the Son of Man (Jesus) coming in His kingdom" (Matthew 16:28).**

The verses in Mark and Luke are also very similar. They all appear to say that Judgement Day and the Second Coming of Jesus would be relatively imminent. It sounded as if Jesus would return within their lifetime. In short, it seems clear that Paul and other Christians expected Jesus to return before they "…tasted death." After all, Jesus said that some of those people from A.D. 29 to A.D. 32 would still be alive when he returned. Within this context, these verses seem to indicate that Jesus had either been misquoted or that he was simply wrong—since all those standing before Jesus nearly 2,000 years ago are all long dead, and Jesus has still not yet returned.

Many Fundamentalist Christians now say that Jesus' kingdom is not a physical kingdom at all, and that his coming would occur within the heart and soul of man. This is entirely possible, and I'll not attempt to argue this point, but it's ironic that this particular ideology is more of a mystical Christian Gnostic teaching that the Apostle Paul would surely have fought against.

Subsequently, we now need to look at some of the very significant problems that are caused by the writings attributed to the Apostle Paul and the Disciple John. These two authors, in particular, dramatically differ from the overall uniformity of the rest of the New Testament. Since over 50% of the New Testament is dominated by Paul and John, it becomes extremely important to understand that the Apostle Paul had never met or heard Jesus teach, and the Disciple John tells a story that is so significantly different from the other disciples that we must seriously question the validity of his writings.

7

The Problem With Paul And John (And President G. W. Bush)

According to the Gospels, there is little question as to Jesus of Nazareth being the Messiah or the Christ, but it is important to understand that the Messiah is not considered God. Throughout the Old Testament, the Messiah is only considered an Anointed One of God. According to the Synoptic texts of Matthew, Mark, and Luke, Jesus also never specifically teaches that he was the Son of God. This is not to say that he wasn't the Son of God. It's just that Jesus never seems to have publicly made this claim himself. Jesus also never teaches that he needed to die for our sins so that we could go to heaven, except in the Gospel of John.

The Apostle Paul, whose New Testament writings seem to predate the Greek translation of the Gospel of John—but unfortunately had never met or personally heard Jesus teach—also began spreading the salvation and divinity message of Jesus (as well as the concept of eternal life through Jesus) not long after his dramatic conversion to Christianity. While traveling on a road to a town called Damascus, Paul (known as Saul prior to his conversion) was temporarily blinded by a brilliant light and heard a voice telling him it was Jesus. This experience so shook up Saul that he converted from Judaism to Christianity, changed his name to Paul, and is now basically credited for spreading Christianity throughout the Roman Empire and to the rest of the world. This life altering experience for Paul occurred in approximately A.D. 36, several years after Jesus' crucifixion. Once again, this is truly unfortunate since Paul, on whom modern day Christianity basically hinges, had never even met Jesus or heard him teach.

Furthermore, in contrast to Jesus' teachings, Paul was very much concerned with the divinity aspect of Jesus and wrote various letters to the scattered Christian churches of the first century with this subject in mind. These thirteen letters, which are all attributed to Paul, make up nearly 50% of the twenty-seven books of the New Testament (some more liberal scholars state that Paul only wrote seven or eight of these letters; nevertheless, the letters are all "Paulian" in nature and bear his name as the author). These letters, or epistles, were also written to encourage Christians to stay faithful since various doubts and changes in Christian doctrine had begun to arise. Nevertheless, it was not until the middle of the second century (nearly 120 years after Jesus was crucified) that these epistles had finally become a part of regular church worship, and it wasn't until the fourth century that these epistles had ultimately become a part of the official canon of the New Testament.

In any case, there is little doubt—by the nature of Paul's letters—that he was expecting Jesus to return in his lifetime. Paul even tries to calm the concerns of other Christians who were worried about dying before Jesus returned. Paul wanted to clarify that Christians would not have to worry. They would ultimately awaken from their graves ("those asleep in Jesus") when Jesus returned on Judgement Day (1 Thessalonians 4:14-18):

> "...God will bring with Him those who sleep in Jesus. For this we say to you by the wound of the Lord, that we who are alive and remain until the coming of the Lord will by no means precede those who are asleep" (NKJV).

As mentioned, Paul initially believed that Jesus would be coming back in his lifetime, but as with many other early Christians, Paul may have come to believe this from the oral Gospel of Matthew that had been circulating for some time (or as mentioned in Chapter 4, from a lost Aramaic written text that was eventually translated into Greek somewhere around A.D. 70 or later). Since the oral tradition was something of a sacred task for many, and as there were others who would know if the original story had changed, the oral Gospel of Matthew ultimately became the written text that bears his name. Paul, therefore, would certainly have been familiar with the concepts reflected in such the verses as Matthew 24:29-35 and Matthew 16:27-28:

> Assuredly, I say to you, this generation will by no means pass away till all these things are fulfilled (Matthew 24:34, NKJV).

> Jesus said "Assuredly, I say to you, there are some standing here who shall not taste death till they see the Son of Man (Jesus) coming in His kingdom" (Matthew 16:28, NKJV].

In the verses of Matthew 24:29-31, Jesus also describes his glorious return to Earth from Heaven. According to Matthew, Jesus states that first century Christians (those who were alive from that generation) would still be around when Jesus did ultimately return. Paul should have been familiar with Matthew's oral rendition of how Jesus would descend from the clouds of Heaven during the final tribulation that occurs at the end of times. Paul's letters reflect this. He's always encouraging Christians to be faithful and ever ready for Jesus' return. Paul even states that Jesus could come at any moment as if **"...a thief in the night" (1 Thessalonians 5:4, NKJV)** had arrived without anyone being ready for it. Paul wanted everyone to be vigilant. He warned everyone not to wait until the last minute to prepare for the return of Jesus. Subsequently, most early Christians had come to believe that Jesus was going to return soon. Scholars also realize that Paul's letters have a certain urgency and an almost frantic aspect to them, and seen through the eyes of Paul, the world appeared to be on the brink of the pro-verbial end of times. Nevertheless, as Paul grew older, his expectations changed. Paul finally realized that Jesus was probably **not** going to return in his lifetime (Wilson 1997).

This is also true of subsequent generations of Christians who also come to realize that Jesus is probably not going to return in their lifetime either. Paul's charismatic writings initially have that effect on people. Paul was so sure that Jesus would be returning soon, that he had other Christians believing the same thing. This applies to Christians of yesterday and today. In the best sense of the term, Paul is a top notch "motivational speaker." It is partly because of Paul's impassioned and ardent writings that Christians of almost every era, including our own, come to believe that Jesus will be returning in their generation. Even the Fundamentalist Christian of today believes that we're living in those final days. These end of times are specifically depicted in the last book of the New Testament, *The Revelation*, which was written by John (or at the very least attributed to him).

With all due respect to the Apostle Paul and the Disciple John, they have both inadvertently served as the catalyst for such misguided fanaticism as The Inquisition and the killing of people in the name of Jesus. Paul and John can also be credited with centuries of misguided Christian zealousness that has been perpetu-ated and reinforced by their enthusiastic and passionate writings. What they wrote was clearly meant for first century Christians, and just as Paul and John enthusiastically fired up these ancient people, nearly every generation of Christians over the last 2,000 years has reacted in a similar capacity. Modern day Christians are no exception. Even today, John and Paul are frequently quoted by

Fundamentalist Christians. Yet for every generation of Christians, it seems that *The Revelation's* description of war, violence, plague, and evil are seen as validation that their era is the final one. The tribulations of mankind, however, have been around for as long as mankind itself. There is nothing new about the horrors that beset the world. Hitler was even seen by some as the Antichrist described in the book of *The Revelation*. Therefore, almost every generation of Christian Fundamentalists grows up believing that their lifetime may be the final one. This time, however, the potential for them being correct is perhaps greater than at any other time in history. The world has far more powerful weapons. Nuclear devices can devastate the Earth. Biological weapons can decimate human populations.

Today's Fundamentalist Christian, therefore, believes that Jesus' return is more imminent than ever before. They are once again using Paul and John's writings to prove that these are the final days prior to Jesus' return. As a matter of fact, many of today's Fundamentalist Christians are buying books on subjects related to the final apocalyptic days. Authors Tim Lahaye and Jerry B. Jenkins have sold well over 60 million copies of their *Left Behind* series of books that basically describe what will happen prior to, during, and after the "Rapture" and the end of days.

Paul also believed in the Rapture. He initially expected to be alive for it (Wilson 1997, 141-42). In short, the Rapture occurs when Jesus removes all the faithful Christians of Earth prior to the great Tribulation. The horrible worldwide calamities of the Tribulation will last seven years followed by Jesus' return and his 1,000 year rule on Earth. Faithful Christian Fundamentalists who have been removed in the Rapture, however, will be spared the inhumanities of those end of times. The rest of us who remain will basically experience seven years of horror, plagues, and hellish devastation, but the faithful Christian will suddenly disappear into thin air from wherever they might be. They'll simply be removed from the Earth, but no one is sure whether clothing, shoes, pacemakers, or surgical implants will also be "left behind" or if these personal items will also be taken up during the Rapture. It may sound like I'm trying to be humorous, but these topics are actually discussed by Fundamentalist Christians, not at any great length perhaps, but they are discussed nonetheless.

As a side note, those taken up in the Rapture could also include President George W. Bush. After all, he does claim to be a Born Again Christian. This can be somewhat disconcerting since his decisions on war, while President, could lead us closer to events that (at the very least) resemble the end of days and the horrors of the Tribulation. If George W. Bush, as a Born Again Christian, really believes in the Rapture and the end of days, his war making decisions could be affected by such a belief. This is especially true since many Born Again Christians are anxiously and hopefully awaiting the Rapture since it also signals the imminent return of Jesus. For Christian Fundamentalists, therefore, the end of times comes with a joyful bonus. Jesus Christ returns in glory to establish his kingdom on Earth.

With regard to Paul's era, however, the Roman Empire was a violent and brutal place to live. The Romans crucified hundreds of thousands of people. In one case, there is an account of 6,000 prisoners of war being crucified along the Appian Way as part of a victory celebration. In an earlier case, 800 Pharisees were crucified in Jerusalem, and—while they were hanging on the cross—their wives and children were slaughtered (Josephus, Antiquities 12.256). These crucifixions were often done alongside busy thoroughfares where many people would see them. Crucifixions were certainly conducted as punishment, but they were also used as a warning to discourage people from breaking Roman laws or rebelling against the Empire. In many ways, the world of the Roman Empire seemed very much like the descriptions provided in *The Revelation*. The Roman Empire was a cruel and vicious entity that took particular pains to annihilate anyone that posed a threat to the status quo of Rome. The Apostle Paul and the Disciple John, therefore, wrote from and about that time. They looked at the world around them and saw what they thought were the end of times, the coming Tribulation, and the expected return of Jesus. If you were a religious zealot, how could you think otherwise? The problem, of course, with the calamities and inhumanities that beset mankind is that these things have always been here. Every generation has had its own suffering to contend with. Death, pestilence, famine, and war have always been with us. Some historians will even tell you that the world has never been without a war, at any given time, throughout its entire recorded history.

The Apostle Paul also focuses on some seemingly unimportant issues. For example, he writes about hair length and the wearing of head garments (1 Corinthians 11:1-15). Paul states that a man **"...is the image and glory of God"** **(NKJV)** and that a woman is **"...the glory of man"** **(NKJV)**. If a man wears a hat while praying, he dishonors himself and God. A woman dishonors herself by not wearing one. This concept may appear trivial, but Paul's words have conditioned churchgoers for centuries. Women needed to wear a hat or head garment in church. Men needed to remove them. Even today, certainly going back to Victorian times, women wear fancy hats to cover their heads during Sunday church service. Paul even goes so far as to stipulate that long hair on a man dishonors that man (and God) because it covers a man's head just as a head garment would. In contrast, Paul says that long hair on a woman honors that woman.

There's actually something far more intriguing going on here. It's rather subtle. It's not hair length and hat wearing. What's important to understand is that Paul has had such a phenomenally strong motivational effect on Christians, that they've actually taken the time to be concerned with something as trivial as hat wearing and hair length. Not only have Christians been influenced to conform to Paul's opinionated criteria of who can wear a hat in church and how long someone should grow their hair, they have also been influenced to accept Paul's interpretation and understanding of Jesus as "Savior of the World." Not only this, Christians have been profoundly influenced to accept Paul's interpretation on issues as they relate to premarital sex, homosexuality, marriage, and many other matters related to morality. In short, Christians take Paul's dogma very serious. His writings still determine what today's morality should be. This may not be a major problem by itself, but as mentioned earlier in this book, when Christians attempt to politically influence morality—and when politicians attempt to solicit votes based on moral conduct—then the potential influence of Paul's code of ethics can become as compelling as it was when people were tyrannized on issues of sexuality by Christian authorities of the past. This is especially disheartening if Paul's teachings have little to do with Jesus Christ's teachings, once again, on whom Christianity should logically be based.

The Apostle Paul also appears to get bogged down with other seemingly peculiar subjects such as circumcision. Paul states that being circumcised hinders a man from being a Christian (Galatians 5:2-6) since it requires him to keep the whole of God's law. For this reason, according to Paul, a man would simply be far better off being uncircumcised.

It's also clear that Paul believed Jesus died for our sins and that Jesus was the only way we could receive eternal life in Heaven. Paul also believed in the divinity aspect of Jesus. He was, after all, beheaded for these beliefs by the Romans in the mid to late A.D. 60s. Nevertheless, Jesus had never accepted the title of God nor did he ever state that we needed to believe he was sacrificed by God so that our sins could be forgiven. Only Paul and John say this. Instead, Jesus responds to Simon Peter with the following:

"'But who do you say that I am?'

And Simon Peter answered and said, 'You are the Christ, the Son of the Living God.'

Jesus answered and said to him, 'Blessed are you, Simon Bar-Jonah, for flesh and blood has not revealed this to you, but My Father who is in heaven'" (Matthew 16:15-17, NKJV).

The accounts in Luke 9:20 and Mark 8:29 are similar, although Jesus doesn't give any response in Luke and gives a somewhat muted response in Mark by telling the disciples to tell no one about this. Only in Matthew does Peter say that Jesus is the Son of God. In each of the Gospels of Mark and Luke, Peter merely states that Jesus is the Christ, the Messiah.

Jesus also seems frustrated by his core group of followers. The twelve disciples were not educated men. They were not scholars. Except for Matthew who was a tax collector, the only other profession that was recorded in the New Testament for any of the disciples is that of fishermen. These working class, "blue collar" disciples often argued among themselves and did not always grasp the concepts that Jesus was trying to teach them. Nevertheless, the bottom-line New Testament issue isn't whether Jesus is the Son of God. This concept seems to be uniformly accepted throughout the subsequent books of the New Testament. Our question should always be whether Jesus _is_ God and whether Heaven can only be received by believing in Jesus as both God and as our personal Savior. In other words, if we believe Jesus died for our sins, are we subsequently spared eternal damnation and granted a place in Heaven?

With regard to John, his **disturbingly** different account of Jesus is clearly contrasted with those given by the first three Gospels. This is clearly evident in numerous Gospel examples where Jesus consistently backs away from publicity in Matthew, Mark, and Luke, yet does nothing to avoid publicity in the Gospel of John. In the earlier Gospels, for example, Jesus repeatedly tells those he cures to tell no one what he has done:

"As soon as He (Jesus) had spoken, immediately the leprosy left him, and he was cleansed.

And He (Jesus) strictly warned him and sent him away at once.

And He (Jesus) said to him, 'See that you say nothing to anyone; but go your way, show yourself to the priest, and offer for your cleansing those things which Moses commanded, as a testimony to them.'" (Mark 1:42-44, NKJV).

John, however, depicts Jesus as not only attracting attention, but openly doing nothing to avoid this publicity. Once again, remember that John was the last of the Gospels written at the end of the first century. Since the book of John differs so dramatically from Matthew, Luke, and Mark, one must truly question the reliability of the book attributed to him:

> **"But look! He (Jesus) speaks boldly, and they (the Jewish leaders) say nothing to Him. Do the rulers know indeed that this is truly the Christ?" (John 7:26, NKJV).**

Another example in John has Jesus forming a whip of cords and forcefully driving out the moneychangers from the temple (John 2:4-16). This also occurs in Mark 11:15-17, but in Mark it occurs much later in Jesus' ministry, not long before his death. In John it occurs very early on, before John the Baptist is beheaded and shortly after Jesus gathers his first disciples. Therefore, according to John, there is absolutely no question as to Jesus being the Son of God and "World Savior" from the very beginning:

> **"Most assuredly, I say to you, he who hears My word and believes in him who sent Me has everlasting life, and shall not come into judgement, but has passed from death into life" (John 5:24, NKJV).**

> **"For God so loved the world that he gave His only begotten Son, that whoever believes in Him should not perish but have everlasting life (John 3:16, NKJV).**

Furthermore, in the very first chapter of John, a disciple of Jesus tells another man that they have found:

> **"...Him of whom Moses in the law, and also the prophets, wrote—Jesus..." (John 1:45, NKJV).**

In other words, they had found the Messiah. This disciple, Nathaniel, also responds in a typical John-like style after seeing and hearing Jesus speak to him:

> **"Nathaniel answered and said to him, 'Rabbi, You are the Son of God! You are the King of Israel!'" (John 1:49, NKJV).**

In Matthew 8:23-27, Mark 4:35-41, and Luke 8:22-25, the disciples are not as certain. Throughout the first three Gospels, the disciples appear anything but John-like in certainty. For example, Jesus had just calmed a storm while he and his disciples were in a boat. After Jesus rebuked the wind with some words, the storm-tossed seas came to a great calm and the disciples responded in a questioning manner:

> "Who can this be, that even the winds and the sea obey him?" (Matthew 8:27, NKJV).

> "Who can this be, that even the wind and the sea obey him!" (Mark 4:41, NKJV).

> "Who can this be? For He commands even the winds and water, and they obey Him!" (Luke 8:25, NKJV).

What's even more remarkable is that Jesus—according to the Gospels—had already raised a man from the dead prior to the calming of the seas (Luke 7:11-17). Once again, within the first three Gospels, it seems absolutely clear that the disciples were seemingly oblivious to who Jesus was. The disciples in John's Gospel, however, are absolutely certain that Jesus is the Son of God, the Messiah, and that this belief is absolutely necessary for receiving eternal life.

The problem is obvious. John is the only Gospel author who directly claims that belief in Jesus as the Son of God is the prerequisite to receiving eternal life. As a side note, it may be important to know that John may not have written the final version of the book attributed to him. One of John's disciples may have actually completed it for him. This seems corroborated by consistent references of respect that refer to John in the third person as **"…the disciple whom Jesus loved" (John 19:26/John 20:2/John 21:20, NKJV)**. The Gospel of John was also probably written in Ephesus (a seaport in the Roman province of Asia) where approximately sixty years or more had elapsed before the actual Gospel of John had been written. This would be more than enough time for a legendary event to reach epic proportions. Regardless, the message in John's other books or epistles are nearly identical to the message of the Gospel that is given his name. He proclaims Jesus as the Messiah, the Son of God, and as God, and that belief in him is the only means to eternal life (1 John 5:11-13). John is also the individual who first brings up the Trinity aspect of God (1 John 5:7-8).

Simon Peter, another non-Gospel writer and an actual eyewitness disciple of Jesus also speaks about Jesus suffering for our sins (1 Peter 3:18), yet Peter's emphasis (as was Jesus') is that we should put our faith in God:

> **"...with the precious blood of Christ...through Him believe in God, who raised him from the dead and gave him glory, so that your faith and hope are in God" (1 Peter 1:19-21, NKJV).**

In contrast, John once again overemphasizes the divinity and salvation aspect of Jesus:

> **"...that God has given us eternal life, and this life is His Son. He who has the Son has life; and he who does not have the Son of God does not have life. These things I have written to you who believe in the name of the Son of God, that you may know you have eternal life..." (1 John 5:11-13, NKJV).**

As noted, John's account clearly varies from the basic uniformity of the first three Gospels, and Paul had never known, met, or directly heard Jesus teach. This in itself doesn't necessarily discredit John or Paul, but it does lend one to question the overall reliability of their statements. In particular, that if we faithfully believe that Jesus died on the cross as the Son of God, we can avoid eternal damnation. This is a <u>very</u> significant statement. If it is true, we must certainly give it some serious thought. After all, life is a very short period of time. Eternity is forever. On the other hand, Jesus never appears to make this statement himself, and if we are really <u>seriously</u> looking for truth, must we blindly accept John and Paul's statement only because we are fearful of the threat of eternal damnation?

This threat even influences many Christians today, but it may have been created simply to prevent people from moving away from the church. The first century was saturated with many Christian Gnostics who often differed in their beliefs regarding Jesus' divinity and the soon to come resurrection of our bodies into Heaven on Judgement Day. Many Christian Gnostics of the time were extremely mystical, some to phenomenal extremes (Layton 1987). To some overzealous Gnostics, Jesus was only an ordinary man until the spirit of God decided to drop into his body. With this Holy Spirit, Jesus was no longer Jesus the man, but Jesus the bodily vessel for God to walk, talk, and perform miracles in. Some of these Gnostic extremists also believed that the Spirit of God dropped out of Jesus while he was on the cross, hence Jesus' words, **"My God, My God, why have You forsaken Me" (Mark 15:34; NKJV).**

It may also be of interest to note that Jesus had a brother, James the Just, who was also known as James the Less (Matthew 27:56/Mark 15:40/Luke 24:10). James the Just was something of a Gnostic himself. He held to Jewish practices and customs, as did Jesus, while Gentile Christians and the Apostle Paul discarded them. Though not an extremist, James the Just was accepted by many Jewish Christians of the first century. Written documents and translations still exist today—attributed to James—in fragmented and semi-complete form. They were written in Coptic, which is an African, Asian, and Egyptian language form. Some churches, however, won't even acknowledge that Jesus had a brother. This would indicate that the Virgin Mary was no longer a virgin after bearing additional offspring subsequent to Jesus. In any case, James the Just died a martyr's death. He was stoned to death by the Jews in A.D. 62 for religious heresy. His Gospel book, along with many other Gnostic texts, were also ignored by early church leaders.

As mentioned earlier, Gnostic translations include the Gospel of Thomas that bears remarkable similarities to Matthew, Mark, and Luke. The Gospels attributed to Mary Magdalene, James, and many others also make up this extensive collection. The powerful influence of Gnosticism was a very real and distinct threat to Paul and the Christian leaders of the early centuries. This Gnostic influence may be one of the reasons why the threat of eternal damnation had been instituted by the early church. It would certainly help keep Christians from straying from the original concepts of the early developing church.

Regardless, it should now be very much apparent that Paul and John are seriously subject to question. At the very least, we must give them far less credence than Matthew, Mark, and Luke.

8

Eternal Life (No Dogma Please, And Hold The Mustard)

Fortunately, the many discrepancies in the New Testament do not seriously detract from the underlying message of Jesus' words. These words, the *red ink* so to speak, are more or less uniform. According to Luke 10:25-28, Mark 12:28-34, and Matthew 22:34-40, Jesus clearly states what you need to do in order to receive eternal life. Jesus' message is probably expressed best with the following:

(A)

"And behold, a certain lawyer stood up and tested Him, saying, 'Teacher, what shall I do to inherit eternal life?'

He (Jesus) said to him, 'What is written in the law? What is your reading of it?'

So he answered and said, 'You shall love the LORD your God with all your heart, with all your soul, with all your strength, and with all your mind, and your neighbor as yourself.'

And He (Jesus) said, 'You have answered rightly; do this and you will live'" (Luke 10:25-28, NKJV).

(B)

"'…Which is the greatest commandment of all?'

Jesus answered him, '…And you shall love the LORD your God with all your heart, with all your soul, with all your mind, and with all your strength. This is the first commandment. And the second, like it, is this: You shall love your neighbor as yourself. There is no other commandment greater than these.'

> **So the scribe said to Him, 'Well said Teacher. You have spoken the Truth, for there is one God, and there is no other but He...'**
>
> **...So when Jesus saw that he had answered wisely, He said to him, 'You are not far from the kingdom of God'" (Mark 12:28-34, NKJV).**

The passage in Matthew 22:34-40 is also similar, but the characters are different. The most important thing to understand from these three particular passages is that Jesus never says that anyone must believe he's God or the Son of God in order to receive eternal life. Jesus also states the following:

> **"Let us go into the next towns, that I may preach there also, because for this purpose I have come forth" (Mark 1:38, NKJV).**

Jesus' earthly purpose seems clear to him, and the greatest commandment and the way to receive eternal life also seem clear. As mentioned in previous chapters, only the Apostle Paul and the Disciple John focus on the issue that we can only be saved and get to Heaven if we believe that Jesus was "murdered" for our sins. Moreover, if you read any of the books attributed to Jesus' disciples (other than John), none of them bring up the requirement of believing in Jesus as the Son of God to receive eternal life. Regardless, they do still proclaim that Jesus was the Son of God and that he had resurrected from the dead. Certainly this is quite an impressive statement, but it does not mean that you're going to Hell if you don't believe this. Other than this, the message of Jesus' disciples throughout the New Testament is basically a continuation of Jesus' ministry.

The Disciple James, who personally knew Jesus, also goes so far as to say that **"...a man is justified by works, and not by faith only"** (James 2:24, NKJV). James can also take credit for being the very first New Testament book written in approximately A.D. 58. Remember, the closer you get to the actual eyewitnesses and disciples of Jesus—and the closer you get to the time line when Jesus was alive—the more accurate the events and teachings of Jesus should likely become. Furthermore, the Disciple Peter states that God **"...judges according to each one's work..."** (1 Peter 1:17, NKJV). Peter's book also appears to be written within 35 years of Jesus' death in approximately A.D. 64.

Fundamentalist Christians, however, will say that doing good works will earn you no credit whatsoever with God. Believing in Jesus as the Son of God and believing that Jesus died on the cross for our sins is the only way we can receive eternal life. There is simply no other way of getting to Heaven. Everyone else is going to Hell.

Once again, Jesus never says this. He doesn't even readily admit to his disciples in Matthew, Mark, and Luke that he is the Son of God—although the disciples do slowly come to believe this over time. Only in the Gospel of John does everyone know that Jesus is the Son of God, and that we must believe Jesus died for our sins to be saved and receive eternal life. Why is John so different? From one point of view, John appears to be the most fanatical and misguided zealot that we encounter in the New Testament Gospels, or he appears to be the only individual who knows something that the other disciples don't know, or something that the other disciples don't ever talk, preach, or direct their attention toward. If believing in Jesus as the Son of God is the only way to receive eternal life, however, then it seems that Jesus' disciples would have actively promoted this issue—but within the New Testament they do not. Once again, the Gospel of John should always be given far less credence than Matthew, Mark, and Luke since his version of Jesus is so dramatically different.

9

Sex, Marriage, And Homosexuality

Some years ago, I was having dinner at a restaurant with eleven Born Again Christian Fundamentalists. I'd been invited to join them after one of their week-day evening church services. Also within this group was an old friend who had previously introduced me to the woman who would eventually become my wife.

Being something of an outside observer, however, I was able to gradually see the subtle psychological reinforcement that one individual received from the group as a whole. This was something analogous to classical conditioning with Christian-like behavior being reinforced by the actions of others. A strong sense of bonding to one's evangelical peer group called for various Born Again Christian, "Praise God" behavior. There was also a definite inclination to conform to the actions of the group. I could distinctly feel this. It was as if we were all the twelve disciples and I was somehow Judas. I really was making no effort at all to conform to the group on issues related to Jesus and his teachings. I was there to ask questions and not to just agree with everything being said. While conformity is rewarded, non-conformity simply designates you as someone who is lost, who has not yet found Jesus, and who has not yet been saved. In short, there are the saved people of the world and there are the non-saved. Sitting at that dinner table, I was one of the non-saved people of the world.

I also found that the metamorphic process that recent Born Again Christian converts follow is a gradual adaptation to new forms of behavior. This is then reinforced by the evangelical peer group. It is important to note, however, that many individuals do seem to change for the better, sometimes radically. Never-theless, the primary drawback is that Born Again Christians frequently believe their way is the only way, and because of this, they'll go about attempting to con-vert others. This aspect of bringing others to Jesus and helping them become saved is one of the basic teachings and fundamental requirements of their new

44

found evangelical relationship with Christ (it's not a religion that they've joined, Born Again Christians will tell you, it's an actual relationship with Jesus Christ). As mentioned earlier, it's a rather admirable quality for Fundamentalist Christians to want to help you become saved. It's almost a humanitarian gesture on their part. They simply want to help you accept Jesus and receive eternal life in heaven with God.

We discussed many things at that dinner table, but I was initially reluctant to debate these well-meaning people. I really didn't want to shake up anyone's faith. Nevertheless, as soon as they began to ask me about whether I was saved, and whether I wanted to be saved, I began bringing up the various discrepancies and issues that were discussed earlier in this book. We also discussed Christian morality. They responded with various quotes from the Old Testament and with quotations from Paul and John.

I then stated that the validity of the Old Testament was in question along with the biblical scripture from Paul and John (as mentioned in earlier chapters). This seemed to irritate one particular male, in his late twenties, seated at the table. He was a New Yorker with a slight Southern accent (for some reason, many evangelical males seem to develop this southern twang, even if they're from New York City). In any case, all the single women were relatively quiet, but I had a lively one hour long conversation with the young man's cheerful and effervescent wife, with periodic Amen's and Praise God's from the others. After I brought up various biblical discrepancies, to which no appropriate or definitive response was given, I was finally asked, "…isn't it better to be safe than sorry, to believe in Jesus as the Son of God than to be uncertain and risk going to Hell?"

It had been a good question, but I honestly responded "…is it better to believe an illusion, in something that is not truth, only to have false peace of mind?" That answer brought a lull of silence and prompted a slightly negative stare or two. I tried to be as diplomatic as possible, but in essence, I was suggesting that they may have deluded themselves into believing something that wasn't true, just to create a false peace of mind. I then brought up the issue of premarital sex. I asked her to show me where in the Synoptic Gospels of Matthew, Mark, and Luke did Jesus say premarital sex was wrong. She gave examples from Paul instead. I asked her again, "Where did **Jesus** say that premarital sex was wrong?" She then replied with the following quotation from Jesus:

> **"You have heard that it was said to those of old, 'You shall not commit adultery.' But I say to you that whoever looks at a women to lust for her**

has already committed adultery with her in his heart" (Matthew 5:27-28, NKJV).

I told her that this particular biblical passage was somewhat ambiguous and could apply to married couples only. The context of the verse itself seemed to verify this. In reply, I opened my Bible to the dictionary section and read the definition of adultery: "Unchastity; unfaithfulness to one's husband or wife" (Dictionary Section, p.2, NKJV). I agreed that **"…what God has joined together, let no man separate" (Mark 10:9, NKJV),** and if a man was joined to his wife by marriage before God and then thought about indulging in sex with another woman, then this could very well be interpreted by Jesus as adultery. It wouldn't hold up in a court of law, but regarding the aspect of a holy and God-consecrated marriage, it seems like something Jesus would have said.

Nevertheless, I was not shown any other red ink biblical words of Jesus that substantiated the sin of adultery while unmarried, except in divorced individuals remarrying. I asked, "…where does Jesus say that if two people really love each other and have premarital relations, that these two are sinning against God. Isn't there enough hate in this world? If two people are expressing the "god-given gift" of physical love, would God really call this wrong?"

Her answer was yes, but it was not a cold heartless response. The tone of voice had been more like faithful adherence to a moral tenet of legality. My point, however, was not to promote the concept of promiscuous behavior. I think enough evidence supports the notion that nature had not meant for men and women to arbitrarily indulge in sex whenever and with whoever they wanted. The fact that venereal disease and hepatitis has been around for ages, that herpes still plagues many individuals today, and that AIDS was apparently introduced as a sexually transmitted disease lends credence to the theory that man was not meant to overindulge in this natural biological function.

It seems more likely that the commandment against adultery was instituted because of logical observation and practicalism, which was reflective of the Jewish people. The Jews may have noted that many promiscuous individuals were suffering the effects of venereal disease—or some facsimile to this—in the same way they noted that eating pork or shellfish could make one ill, or how some uncircumcised children were acquiring genital diseases. As with any ancient people, there were some who gradually implemented practical observation into their religion. In any case, premarital sex did not seem to be a great concern or a primary issue for Jesus, only the abuse of it, specifically for those individuals who were married before God.

Subsequently, Christian morality has clearly evolved into something that is far more encompassing than anything Jesus had ever discussed with his disciples. Christian morality, as we know it today, almost entirely stems from the Apostle Paul and his interpretation of what morality should be. Paul's attitude toward marriage was also influenced by his belief that Jesus was about to return. He even suggested that if Christians could hold out for the Rapture, they might be better off staying celibate. In addition, although Paul's condemnation of homosexuals has had a widespread and deleterious effect on the modern day Christian's acceptance of this lifestyle, he really wasn't trying to set up the rules of morality for future generations of Christians. Paul was simply preparing everyone for the imminent return of Jesus Christ. Believing that Jesus was about to return, and that the Tribulation would begin soon, Paul felt that everyone would be far better off being celibate. After all, the ideal was to be taken up in the Rapture and to avoid the calamities, suffering, and horrors of the Tribulation and the end of times.

Furthermore, during a time when homosexual behavior was quite common in the Greek and Roman world—Emperor Claudius was actually considered rather eccentric for only liking women—Paul felt that an individual would be far better off simply avoiding any sexual behavior, particularly homosexuality. Paul's criticism of homosexuals also stemmed from a puritanical strain of Old Testament thinking that, for whatever reason, Paul simply adopted as his own (Wilson 1997). Some could even say that Paul projected an image that was somewhat homophobic. I won't try to prove or disprove this possibility. It's sufficient to say that Paul clearly did not approve of the lifestyle. As for Jesus, there is absolutely no biblical text that has him ever discussing the subject of homosexuality on any level at any time, although the Old Testament does basically forbid this type of behavior. Subsequently, let's now take a brief look at the Old Testament as a possible and viable source for Christian morality.

10

The Old Testament As A Source (Cut Off The Hands Of "Them" Women)

I realize that it's somewhat difficult, if not impossible, for many Christian Fundamentalists to discard the infallibility of the Old Testament. The Old Testament prophecies have been used to verify the fulfillment of Jesus as the promised Messiah of the Jewish people. It is also important to note that the term Christ simply translates as Messiah, which means The Anointed One of God. It does not translate as God or Son of God. The Messiah was specifically anointed by God to save the people of Israel in the last days. In short, Christianity can be somewhat accurately described as a form of Jewish "Messiahism."

In order to show reasons for questioning the validity of the Old Testament, we need to look at several examples of why it may not be as reliable a guide as many Christian authorities may ask us to believe. One example that sheds some light on this validity is found in Leviticus, where an argument can be made about God's acceptance of slavery for his chosen people of Israel:

> **"And as for your male and female slaves whom you may have—from the nations that are around you, from them you may buy male and female slaves. Moreover you may buy the children of the strangers who sojourn among you, and their families who are with you, which they beget in your land; and they shall become your property. And you may take them as an inheritance for your children after you, to inherit them as a possession; they shall be your permanent slaves" (Leviticus 25:44-46, NKJV).**

Many African countries occupy the land south of Israel, and I find it difficult to conceive of God condoning the practice of owning black slaves or even white slaves for that matter. Another example in Deuteronomy 23:1-2 has God forbidding men with injured or damaged genitals from joining a congregation of the Lord. Illegitimate children are also not allowed. Even the descendants of these illegitimate children are not allowed for up to ten generations afterwards. Furthermore, in the Old Testament book of Deuteronomy, when two men are fighting, and one man's wife tries to help her husband by seizing the genitals of her husband's enemy, her hand is to be cut off without mercy:

> **"If two men fight together, and the wife of one draws near to rescue her husband from the hand of the one attacking him, and puts out her hand and seizes him by the genitals, then you shall cut off her hand; your eye shall not pity her" Deuteronomy 25:11-12, NKJV).**

Are these the words of God? I'm by no means attempting to be clever. I always find these types of biblical verses very interesting. Logic, however, would dictate that Old Testament morality was simply reflective of the harsh and difficult times the ancient Hebrew people lived in. Humankind evolves. Laws evolve. Nevertheless, there are some individuals who still believe in the applicability of these ancient Old Testament teachings. Some might even suggest that we begin cutting off the hands of women who find themselves in similar situations today. For some Christians, after all, the Bible is the "true infallible Word of God." In contrast, many Protestants and Catholics accept parts of the Bible as stories with a lesson, often about morality. Yet many Fundamentalist Christians assume that everything in the Bible should be taken literally. This, unfortunately, can often lead to the various strict and dogmatic views of what Christian morality and ethics should be.

With regard to historical facts, Old Testament biblical chronology and available historical facts appear to correlate. Although there are some problems with the Old Testament, chronological charts created from ancient biblical texts have basically shown themselves to be accurate (Finegan 1964). They depict a fairly reliable history. This doesn't discard the notion that fiction was also incorporated into the Old Testament. This is similar in analogy to Homer's mythical cities and events that were later discovered to have existed in the archaeological past, yet much myth was also incorporated into these ancient Greek writings. In my recent encounters with certain Christian Fundamentalist groups, however, I would get a definitive answer that absolutely everything in the Bible is true. This includes the belief that biblical chronology showing the world to be less than 6,000 years old, traced back to the original Adam and Eve, is absolute and total fact.

Furthermore, and contrary to the ideology of a constant and all-knowing God, it appears that a type of spiritual evolution occurs with the Old Testament God. Yahweh or Jehovah (JHWH, Semitic words omit vowels) appears to become considerably more compassionate. He also becomes less bloodthirsty and vengeful against the enemies of Israel and even against Israel herself. This biblical evolution of God seems to advance to the point where he mercifully sends his only begotten son into the world to save it according to mainstream Christianity (John 3:16). This, of course, is not accepted by the Jewish faith. For Jews, the Old Testament is still an unfinished book awaiting a Messiah to fulfill its prophecies. Subsequently, let's now take a look at some of the ancient prophecies that many Christians say Jesus fulfills. These Old Testament prophecies help explain how and why Jesus was accepted as the Messiah by his followers.

11

Biblical Prophecy Of The Messiah Fulfilled?

Several passages are used by Christians to show that Jesus fulfills the ancient prophecies of the Messiah. These prophecies correspond rather strikingly at times to the life and death of Jesus. The following quote from Psalms has been dated at approximately 1045 B.C. The second quote is from Isaiah and has been dated at approximately 700 B.C. Since both of these passages have been used for centuries to prove that Jesus fulfills the ancient Old Testament prophecies, I have used the translations from the original King James Bible. The following verses from Psalms 22:1-21 bear noticeable similarity to events occurring more than 1,000 years later. In particular, note the underlined print:

[1] <u>My God, my God, why hast thou forsaken me?</u> why art thou so far from helping me, and from the words of my roaring?
[2] O my God, I cry in the daytime, but thou hearest not; and in the night season, and am not silent.
[3] But thou art holy, O thou that inhabitest the praises of Israel.
[4] Our fathers trusted in thee: they trusted, and thou didst deliver them.
[5] They cried unto thee, and were delivered: they trusted in thee, and were not confounded.
[6] <u>But I am a worm, and no man; a reproach of men, and despised of the people.</u>
[7] <u>All they that see me laugh me to scorn: they shoot out the lip, they shake the head saying,</u>
[8] <u>He trusted on the LORD that he would deliver him: let him deliver him, seeing he delighted in him.</u>
[9] But thou art he that took me out of the womb: thou didst make me hope when I was upon my mother's breasts.
[10] I was cast upon thee from the womb: thou art my God from my mother's belly.
[11] Be not far from me; for trouble is near; for there is none to help.

[12] Many bulls have compassed me: strong bulls of Bashan have beset me round.
[13] They gaped upon me with their mouths, as a ravening and a roaring lion.
[14] I am poured out like water, and all my bones are out of joint: my heart is like wax; it is melted in the midst of my bowels.
[15] My strength is dried up like a potsherd; and my tongue cleaveth to my jaws; and thou hast brought me into the dust of death.
[16] For dogs have compassed me: the assembly of the wicked have inclosed me: they pierced my hands and my feet.
[17] I may tell all my bones: they look and stare upon me.
[18] They part my garments among them, and cast lots upon my vesture.
[19] But be not thou far from me, O LORD: O my strength, haste thee to help me.
[20] Deliver my soul from the sword; my darling from the power of the dog.
[21] Save me from the lion's mouth: for thou hast heard me from the horns of the unicorns (KJV).

According to the Book of Mark, one of Jesus' last words had been "My God, My God, why have You forsaken me?" (Mark 15:34, NKJV).

Jesus was certainly *despised and scorned*. While on the cross, onlookers stood around gazing and mocking Jesus. "He trusted in God; let HIM deliver Him now if HE will have Him" (Matthew 27:43, NKJV).

Jesus had also hung on a cross for nearly six hours (Mark 15:25-33). Hanging on a cross would logically put Jesus' *bones out of joint.*

According to the New Testament, Jesus had thirsted while hanging on the cross, his *tongue cleaving to his jaw* or his throat. One of the symptoms of crucifixion is dehydration.

They *pierced Jesus' hands and feet* with nails.

The Romans also broke the legs of the two criminals whom Jesus was crucified with (a common practice to expedite death), but according to the New Testament they pierced Jesus' side instead because he was already dead. In this way, his *unbroken bones* could all be counted. Water and blood emerging from his wound might also indicate that his heart had burst, perhaps *melting like wax*, or that his heart had been punctured by the piercing.

The soldiers also took the clothing of Jesus and *cast lots* for his seamless tunic.

Another passage used by Christians to show Jesus fulfilling the prophecy of the Messiah is Isaiah 53:1-12. Here the prophet Isaiah speaks to the Jewish people about something known as the Suffering or Martyred Servant. Christians say that it describes Jesus. It also describes how Jesus' people, the Jews, would see and think of him. Again, note the underlined print in particular:

[1] Who hath believed our report? and to whom is the arm of the LORD revealed?

[2] For he shall grow up before him as a tender plant, and as a root out of a dry ground: he hath no form nor comeliness; and when we shall see him, there is no beauty that we should desire him.

[3] He is despised and rejected of men; a man of sorrows, and acquainted with grief: and we hid as it were our faces from him; he was despised, and we esteemed him not.

[4] Surely he hath borne our griefs, and carried our sorrows: yet we did esteem him stricken, smitten of God, and afflicted.

[5] But he was wounded for our transgressions, he was bruised for our iniquities: the chastisement of our peace was upon him; and with his stripes we are healed.

[6] All we like sheep have gone astray; we have turned every one to his own way; and the LORD hath laid on him the iniquity of us all.

[7] He was oppressed, and he was afflicted, yet he opened not his mouth: he is brought as a lamb to the slaughter, and as a sheep before her shearers is dumb, so he openeth not his mouth.

[8] He was taken from prison and from judgment: and who shall declare his generation? for he was cut off out of the land of the living: for the transgression of my people was he stricken.

[9] And he made his grave with the wicked, and with the rich in his death; because he had done no violence, neither was any deceit in his mouth.

[10] Yet it pleased the LORD to bruise him; he hath put him to grief: when thou shalt make his soul an offering for sin, he shall see his seed, he shall prolong his days, and the pleasure of the LORD shall prosper in his hand.

[11] He shall see of the travail of his soul, and shall be satisfied: by his knowledge shall my righteous servant justify many; for he shall bear their iniquities.

[12] Therefore will I divide him a portion with the great, and he shall divide the spoil with the strong; because he hath poured out his soul unto death: and he was numbered with the transgressors; and he bare the sin of many, and made intercession for the transgressors (KJV).

It's true that translating Hebrew into English is not an exact science. Certain Semitic words just don't translate well into English, and the lack of vowels in the Semitic language sometimes proposes a problem. As mentioned, Christians have used these passages to help authenticate the claim that Jesus was the Messiah, but most Jews maintain that the passages are about the people of Israel. In any case,

Jesus appears to fit Isaiah's description, including the fact that he died with criminals and "...*made his grave with the wicked*." He was also buried "...*with the rich in his death*" in the wealthy Joseph of Arimathea's tomb.

Other Old Testament prophecies include the concept of the Messiah being born of a virgin (Isaiah 7:14), but translation error may have taken place related to this word. The word *alma* is the actual word used in the original Hebrew text. *Alma* has several meanings. It can basically describe a young woman who was recently married or it can mean an actual virgin. The exact word in Hebrew that would have described a virgin is *bethula*. During the first Hebrew to Greek translations, the Hebrew *alma* was incorrectly translated into Greek as *parthenos* (which has the explicit meaning of a virgin). The Greek word *neanis* should have been used since it corresponds most closely to the Hebrew word *alma*.

The Messiah, therefore, didn't have to be born of a virgin in the strictest sense of the word (*bethula*), but he could have been born from a recently married young woman or a virgin (*alma*). Subsequently, the Gospels may have been shaped around the concept of a virgin birth to emphasize prophetic fulfillment. This is not to say that Mary wasn't a virgin, but this need not detract from the concept of Jesus being the Anointed One of God if he had **not** been born of a virgin. It will, however, cause problems for those who insist that Jesus could only have been the Messiah if the Virgin Mary had been impregnated by God himself.

According to some Christians, there are as many as 425 prophecies of the Messiah in the Old Testament. Some are ambiguous at best. Others are extremely interesting at the very least. One ancient prophecy, which is apparently fulfilled by Jesus, includes the prediction that the Messiah would be born in Bethlehem (Micah 5:1-2). According to the New Testament, Jesus was born in Bethlehem. Another prophecy says the Messiah would be a man of peace (Micah 5:2-5). According to the New Testament, Jesus was a man of peace. Ancient prophecy also states that the Messiah would teach in Galilee (Isaiah 9:1-2). According to the New Testament, Jesus did teach in Galilee.

As mentioned earlier, some critics say that the Gospels were molded around the Old Testament prophecies. Others such as Hugh J. Schonfield say that Jesus meticulously went about deliberately fulfilling prophecy—not because he **was** the Messiah—but because Jesus **thought** he was the Messiah and therefore needed to accomplish certain things that fulfilled the ancient prophecies. Mr. Schonfield often presents a very plausible argument in his book, *The Passover Plot*, although he sometimes goes too far in his speculations. For example, he theorizes that Jesus might have been drugged on the cross to simulate death. He also suggests that a follower might have impersonated Jesus after his crucifixion. Regardless, while

Mr. Schonfield does portray Jesus as an exceptional individual, he also indicates that Jesus might have had one very significant flaw. He speculates that Jesus simply had the misguided and false notion that he was actually the Messiah.

It seems somewhat difficult to believe, however, that the disciples would go to such great trouble—and with such considerable risk to their lives by the Romans and the Jews—to establish and then maintain the hoax of falsifying the resurrection of Jesus and then promoting him as the Messiah. The disciple Peter was even crucified upside down in Rome, in A.D. 64 or A.D. 67, for spreading the teachings of Jesus. He was crucified in this manner because he didn't want the honor of dying the same way Jesus had. With regard to Jesus, Peter says the following:

> **"Blessed be the God and Father of our Lord Jesus Christ, who according to His abundant mercy has begotten us again to a living hope through the resurrection of Jesus Christ from the dead" (1 Peter 1:3, NKJV).**

> **"For we did not follow cunningly devised fables when we made known to you the power and coming of our Lord Jesus Christ, but were eyewitnesses of his majesty. For He received from God the Father honor and glory when such a voice came to him from the Excellent Glory: 'This is my beloved Son, in whom I am well pleased.' And we heard this voice which came from heaven when we were with Him on the holy mountain" (2 Peter 1:16-18, NKJV).**

I'm always impressed with the fact that Peter had been an actual eyewitness of Jesus, was an actual author of the books attributed to him, had recognized Jesus as the Messiah, had proclaimed him to be the Son of God, and was willing to die a horrible death in order to tell others this message. This does not seem to logically befit the actions of an individual intending to spread false propaganda for his own benefit.

From New Testament records, it does seem possible that Jesus might have been **a** *Son of God*, and maybe he was even **the** *Son of God*. What is more clear, however, is that many of Jesus' teachings have been elaborated on by well meaning Christians such as Paul and John. Once again, for something to be called genuine Christianity, it seems that the religion should be based on the actual teachings of Jesus Christ. Otherwise why even call it Christianity? You might as well call it Paulism or Johnism.

As for the belief in Jesus' death being a prerequisite for eternal life, only John and Paul focus in on this issue. Jesus seems to have had a very different message for humankind. Unfortunately, this message was sometimes poorly and inadequately captured by the New Testament authors, but even though Jesus never wrote anything himself, his message may be best conveyed by his distinct example of love, compassion, and forgiveness.

As a matter of fact, of all things we know about Jesus in the New Testament, **(1) love, (2) compassion, and (3) forgiveness** are the three things that immediately stand out about him. Jesus also wanted to let us know that we could directly speak to God without an intermediary such as a priest, monk, or rabbi. He did this when he taught his disciples the *Lord's Prayer*. Jesus also seemed to want to make known that there was a life beyond this one. If there was no other life after this life, why bother resurrecting from the dead? Lastly, Jesus wanted to tell us that we should always love and trust in God above all things.

Of course, the New Testament can be viewed by some as fictional literature, but Peter's eyewitness account and his subsequent crucifixion tend to be the two primary aspects that prompt me to believe otherwise. Furthermore, if Peter had really denied on three separate occasions that he knew Jesus (Matthew 26:34/ Mark 14:30/Luke 22:34/John 13:38), then when Peter had the opportunity to deny Jesus again and be spared a brutal and excruciatingly abhorrent crucifixion, I believe he would have done so if Jesus' resurrection had all been a hoax. Otherwise what in the world was the purpose of being crucified upside down to a cross? Why wouldn't Peter simply deny Jesus again?

To summarize, Matthew, Mark, and Luke tend to synoptically reflect Jesus' teachings. It is this uniformity that gives these texts greater significance and believability. Scholarly evidence also encourages us to read Matthew and Mark with greater depth because Matthew appears to be translated from an original Aramaic text, and Mark is very likely to be the very first Greek translation.

With regard to John, can we really take him seriously? The Gospel of John simply differs far too dramatically from Matthew, Mark, and Luke. With regard to Paul, he also appears to have gotten some of his wires crossed. This includes Paul's mistaken notion that Jesus was going to return in his lifetime. More importantly, Paul had never met Jesus and had therefore never heard Jesus teach. For these reasons and others, reading anything in the New Testament by either Paul or John should always be done with a certain amount of skepticism. On the other hand, Jesus' words in Matthew, Mark, and Luke should always be read thoroughly and be given the highest emphasis.

It is also quite clear that the New Testament has its flaws, and various church dogma should always be considered in this light. In other words, whenever evaluating any doctrine of Christianity, one should always compare it to words of Jesus Christ in the Synoptic texts of Matthew, Mark, and Luke. Christian Fundamentalists, for example, have evolved their own variations of dogma that are based primarily on Paul. They then spend a good deal of time teaching about the false dogma of other Christian and non-Christian cults. The Mormons, Jehovah Witnesses, and Buddhists are considered to be some of these cults. Frequently, you will hear about what's wrong with these religions rather than teaching the actual message of Jesus. I've also noticed, first hand, a lot of criticism directed toward Catholics on such issues as faith and prayer to Mary and other saints. Christian Fundamentalists also spend far too much time criticizing Catholicism's emphasis on morality, rather than salvation, while at the same time promoting Paul's very dogmatic interpretation of Christian morality, which clearly chastises adulterers and homosexuals.

What comes to mind is a quotation from Mark 9:40 where Jesus specifically tells the Disciple John, **"For he who is not against us is on our side" (NKJV).** John was told this because he had forbidden others to do good works in the name of Jesus, simply because these other people were not direct followers of the twelve disciples. Once again, this is just another example of how John sometimes miscalculated where Jesus was coming from. In this particular case, John had not understood the acceptance that Jesus had for ALL people who were seeking God and who were trying to do positive things in his name.

Subsequently, with regard to some of these non-Christians who seem to fall into the category of **"For he who is not against us is on our side" (NKJV)**, let's now take a look at *Jesus, Buddhism, and Kabbalah*.

12

Jesus, Buddhism, And Kabbalah (A Brief Comparison)

It is obvious that Jesus of Nazareth had a tremendous impact on the world of the Roman Empire nearly 2,000 years ago. He still has a tremendous effect on people today. It is also important to note that the biblical Jesus never really states that belief in him as God, or as the Son of God, was a requirement for eternal life, except for the contradictory indications in John. The Apostle Paul also seems to incorrectly focus on this issue. In contrast, Jesus' message was very simple:

    (1) Love God with all your heart, soul, and mind.
    (2) Do to others only what you would have them do to you.
    (3) Do not judge others or you'll risk judgement upon yourself.
    (4) Love your neighbor as yourself.

Using one of his numerous parables, Jesus also showed a great deal of mercy and lenience to unknowing sinners:

> **"But he who did not know, yet committed things worthy of stripes, shall he be beaten with few." But, "For everyone to whom much is given, from him much will be required…" (Luke 12:48, NKJV).**

If Jesus wasn't the Messiah or the Son of God, he still seemed to project an extraordinary godlike image reflected by great love, compassion, and wisdom; however, if Jesus really is the Messiah or the Son of God—and if his compassion reflects even a part of what God is really like—then we as human beings may have a relatively good idea of what we need to do. We simply need to follow the example of Jesus.

Sometimes Christians also forget that Jesus was born a Jew. According to the New Testament, Jesus celebrated Passover and followed most of the Jewish traditions. Jesus had also studied Judaism. In fact, he was found in the temple with Jewish elders when he was just a child. There are also some who say that Jesus studied Buddhism between the ages of thirteen and twenty-nine. The New Testament makes no reference to Jesus during this period of time. It's almost as if Jesus disappears from the face of the Earth until he emerges, once again, in the public eye at the age twenty-nine.

Ancient Buddhist records may actually explain this gap of time. These texts refer to an individual known as Issa from Palestine who journeyed from Jerusalem to India and studied with Buddhist and Hindu holy men. These ancient scrolls were first discovered and reviewed by Nicolas Notovitch in 1894. They are reported in his book, *The Unknown Life of Christ.* It may also be interesting to note that the name, Issa, is the name given to Jesus in the Muslim scriptural text known as the Koran.

In any case, Jesus' teachings often seem Buddhist in nature, but according to some modern day Kabbalists—an ancient Jewish Mysticism enjoying a modern resurgence of worldwide popularity—Kabbalah was the early influence for all these far eastern religions. Kabbalah is mentioned in the Koran, and it had even influenced the development of Hinduism and Buddhism. For example, Abraham's *Book of Formation*, the first written work on Kabbalah, occurred approximately 4,000 years ago in 2000 B.C.E. This written work is said to contain all of the mysteries of the universe. This might explain why many of Jesus' teachings also appear Kabbalistic in nature. According to Yehuda Berg, author of *The Power of Kabbalah*, Jesus did in fact study Kabbalah:

> **"He learned the Kabbalistic technique of ritual immersion in water and Kabbalistic meditation from *Jochanan the Immerser* (John the Baptist). In the Gospels of Thomas, which contain Jesus' secret teachings given to only his closest disciples, he teaches that light is the origin of all humanity and that each person is a spark of the Divine. All people are considered, 'children of the Light.' It was Kabbalah that he used to perform acts of healing and other wonders" (page 234).**

> **"...the death of a great Kabbalistic sage helps to purify and cleanse the sins of his or her generation. Consequently, Kabbalists understand that these great souls were also killed to cleanse the sins of their fellow Israelites...These great Kabbalistic sages were considered to be 'Sons of God.' In fact, the Zohar says that anyone who studies its Kabbalistic wisdom is called 'the Son of the Holy One' (Son of God) and 'the Son of the Father'"(page 234-235).**

Regardless of whether Jesus studied the Kabbalah or whether he was the Issa of ancient Buddhist records, his teachings are very much Buddhist in nature on such key issues as a nonviolent approach to life. According to the Buddhist monks of the famous Chuang Yen Monastery in Carmel, New York, some sayings that have been attributed to Chinese and Tibetan Buddhism that find great similarity to Jesus' teachings include the following:

<u>Some Sample Sayings of the Buddha</u>

One Who Sees My Teachings Sees Me.

One Who Serves The Sick Serves Me.

Hatred Cannot Be Appeased By Hatred. Hatred Can Only Be Appeased By Love.

One Should Neither Kill Nor Cause To Kill.

The Evil Doer Grieves Here And Hereafter.

Blessed Are They Who Earn Their Living Without Hurting Others.

Radiate Your Loving Kindness To Every Living Being Without Discrimination.

As You Sow Shall You Reap.

Do Not Deceive Others.

Do Not Despise Any Person Anywhere.

Hide Your Good Deeds, Confess Before The World The Sins You Have Committed.

Radiate Your Loving Kindness To Every Living Being Without Any Discrimination.

Do Good, Do No Evil, And Purify Yourself.

Go Forth In The World, For The Good Of The Many And The Welfare Of The Many.

Always Try To Acquire Wisdom, Practice, Devotion, Morality, And Charity.

Furthermore, according to the Buddhist holy book, *The Somadeva*, there is a written account of a Buddhist monk whose eye had "offended him" so he plucked it out and cast it away. Jesus also taught "**And if your right eye causes you to sin, pluck it out and cast it from you**" **(Matthew 5:29, NKJV).**

Other similarities include the notion that Jesus Christ and The Buddha both went to their temples at the age of twelve and astonished all those who were there. Both began their ministries at approximately the same ages (Jesus at thirty; The Buddha at twenty-nine). Both have stories about being tempted by the Devil at the very beginning of their ministries. They both have narratives about wandering to a fig tree at the conclusion of their fasts. Both fasted in solitude for long periods of time (Jesus for forty days; The Buddha for forty-seven). Both are also said to have known the thoughts of others and to know what was in their hearts.

Many Buddhist parables and legends even sound as if they had been taken right out of the New Testament, but these Buddhist stories and anecdotes predate Christianity. Buddhism was founded in approximately 588 B.C. Subsequently, Christianity may have "borrowed" some of these Buddhist stories and applied them to Jesus. As a matter of fact, Christian morality and related teachings contain a great number of similarities to Buddhism. Again, this is really not that unusual since Buddhism is five centuries older than Christianity. This Far East religion had already spread through most of India and Ceylon, and had also expanded into China and Central Asia, by the time Jesus was born.

Regardless, the speculations of whether Jesus traveled to the Far East and studied Buddhism is not overly important, but it is interesting to examine and evaluate such a possibility. The fact of the matter is that almost all great spiritual teachers have similar teachings. Other than the deity aspect of Jesus—which was basically ascribed to Jesus by others—the teachings of Jesus and all great teachers from Buddha to Krishna to Moses to Mohammed all have significantly interesting similarities.

Let's now take a brief look at *Science, Disillusionment, and the Existence of God.* This is somewhat important since a theory is also proposed in the Epilogue that discusses *Astrophysics, Karma, And How Everything In The Universe May Actually Work* that connects Jesus with such concepts as Science, Astronomy, Physics, Astrophysics, Karma, Kabbalah, and even Reincarnation.

13

Science, Disillusionment, And The Existence Of God

Science has often been criticized in that it undermines the existence of God. Science, however, does not undermine this belief. Even more precisely, science cannot undermine a belief in God. Life itself has a tendency to accomplish this task alone. The struggles that occur in daily existence, the mundane aspects of our world, and the pains that each of us encounter seem to often weaken or destroy our belief in any kind of God.

If we look at science, Astronomy in particular, we can see the fantastic beauty of this universe. One look at a clear winter night sky with a high powered telescope or a set of binoculars, away from the bright lights of a city, we can see sparkling red giants such as Betelgeuse in Orion, hot blue stars like Sirius, binary and triple stars, galaxies, exploded star nebulas, and even some common medium sized yellow stars like our own.

Moreover, if Astronomy studies the complexities of the universal macrocosm, then Chemistry examines the intricacies of the universal microcosm. Both are uniquely complicated as well as ultimately simple. From time to time, these various sciences can prompt us to wonder if there really is a god like architect behind the creation of this massive universe.

I only say this because the reality of a personalized God seems to elude many of us. Still, there are times when one experiences an incredible peace, of being in touch with something beyond oneself and one's own finite existence. It is then that everything seems to fall into place with the realization that all things have a purpose, and a peaceful almost Christ-like understanding seems to temporarily permeate this material existence.

Science, however, in its role as objective guide to the laws of the physical universe, basically accomplishes its goal. It records data, analyzes information, and comes to logical conclusions and speculative theories. These may change in time as new evidence presents itself. Biology, for example, seems to accomplish this goal. It analyzes data and develops logical conclusions, although it also sometimes promotes its own conclusions and theories as absolute dogma.

Nevertheless, each of the sciences reveals a complexity about life that eventually leads one to see ultimate simplicity within all of the apparent discord. There seems to be an orderly system of cause and effect within this universe that seems to be verified or explained in one way or another by science. In other words, science is only contradictory to religion from those points of view that relate to such things as Evolution or the age of the earth. For example, some Fundamentalist Christians still believe the Earth is less than 6,000 years old and that evolution is a false theory. Others are in disagreement with theoretical explanations provided by psychiatric and psychological schools of thought, rather than solving all your problems through God alone. These discrepancies between science and religious thought in no way need to detract from a belief in God, nor should it, unless one wants it to.

Various scientific studies, including research into individuals' near-death experiences regarding possible life after death, seem to possibly have a basis for validity. On the other hand, researcher Madeleine Griggs' discovery that brain activity continues for an average of 37 hours after death, with the longest dead brain activity continuing for as long as 168 hours (*Science Digest*, April 1988) seems to possibly suggest that near-death religious experiences may merely be a by-product of dying brain activity.

There are also eastern mystics who claim that they can astral travel or soul travel to other planes of existence. This in itself is not really scientific, but science has attempted to understand how some of these individuals can walk on hot coals or sit on beds of sharp nails with little or no pain or harm to themselves.

It is true that, in subtle ways, the concept of a personal God seems weakened by science. The universe is so massive that besides the billions of people who inhabit this small planet Earth (which orbits the Sun at 18 mps; the Sun in turn orbits the Milky Way Galaxy at 135 mps, every 225 to 250 million years or so), other billions of life forms may also exist elsewhere in this galaxy or even in another galaxy. In fact, the universe is so incredibly large that—in our galaxy alone—light takes approximately 100,000 years to travel from one end to the other. Light also takes approximately 2 million years to reach us from one of our neighboring sister galaxies, Andromeda, with light traveling at approximately 186,282 miles per second. According to astronomers, the Andromeda Galaxy is also traveling toward us at 75 miles per second on an apparent collision course that will occur in approximately 6 billion years (i.e., 60 galactic years from now).

According to computer models of stellar evolution, our star will also have exhausted its hydrogen fuel in about 6.2 billion years. The Sun will then begin burning helium and become a Red Giant, expanding to the orbit of Earth. Our Sun will then burn for another 700 million years or so, and when its helium fuel is exhausted, it will eventually become a .55 sized solar white dwarf.

All this being said, it is subsequently possible to assume that this is far too large a universe for God to be everywhere, and that there are just too many people on this planet for God to hear everyone's prayers all the time. It is also possible to conclude that God has created a cause and effect mechanical universe that runs fairly smoothly, and if we really need God, the message supposedly gets through. I seem to have had this fact corroborated by a graduate level university professor who, while grinning as he said it, claimed to have a direct telecommunications link to Heaven itself. He told me with a heavy Irish accent, "God is a bit hard of hearing, you know, so you'd better speak up."

As for Science, and at the risk of sounding redundant, it should not, need not, nor does it necessarily conflict with the concept of a personal God. Cynicism, however, in its various forms can provide one with a disillusionment that is often hard to shake. Life can sometimes make cynics out of the best of us, from Freud to the disgruntled philosopher. Where cynicism exists, a personal God seems to have little access, or perhaps cynicism causes God to become seemingly less obvious in our lives. Whereas science, when it is without this cynicism, simply functions as an exploratory medium, a means for analysis, and an educational vehicle that attempts to fathom and explain the mysteries of this universe.

I'd also like to relate a personal analogy about the actual existence of God. According to science, which often functions as our main authoritative source of truth, almost all things created in a laboratory or elsewhere require an inventor, architect, or creator. If this holds true, then the creation of this massive universe—held together by various Laws of Physics—would logically require a creator. It is so massive a universe, in fact, that for each star we see in the sky, there are an equivalent amount of galaxies that contain hundreds of billions of stars per galaxy (smaller galaxies may only have hundreds of millions of stars). What a truly amazing concept. Billions of galaxies with at least several hundred million stars per galaxy.

Furthermore, even the *Big-Bang Theory*, regarding the initial birth of the universe, might not quite hold up without the concept of a creator. For many years, scientists had only been able to theorize back to a fraction of a second after the *Big Bang*, but no further, and a valid theory for the universe before this event seemed to be beyond anyone's conception. Some astrophysicists, however, have recently theorized that *Big Bangs* may occur in periodic cycles over the course of trillions of years. Although there are variations on the theory, *Big Bangs* may result when two 10-dimensional branes (astrophysicist lingo for membranes: the "walls" on each side of a universe) collide with each other. In one scenario, parallel universes may be located right next to each other, one after another, like slices in a loaf of bread. When one of these universes smacks into or bounces off an adjacent parallel universe, an enormous amount of energy would be released. The energy released from this collision would create a massive sea of quarks, protons, electrons, photons, and other subatomic particles. It creates a *Big Bang* if you will. This can then develop into a type of universe that we live in today. In any case, I'm sure that other scientists will eventually propose additional theories to explain creation from its very absolute beginning, but once again, creation seems to logically require a creator.

Allow me to introduce one last and slightly different analogy. If Jesus' words could be symbolized as two atoms of Hydrogen—one of the single and most important elements in the universe—and when Christian evangelists "air" a somewhat different message symbolized by one atom of Oxygen, then doesn't Jesus' original message change and become watered down (symbolized by H_2O)? This may be a whimsical way of looking at this, but in some ways the analogy seems appropriate. In other words, we must always look at the original message of Jesus Christ in order to find the underlying truth and essence of Christianity, and we must never blindly accept evolving and changing church dogma for the sake of expediency, false peace of mind, or convenience.

Epilogue

✦

Astrophysics, Karma, And How Everything In The Universe May Actually Work

If you're interested in a little speculation on how life may really work in conjunction with how the universe may really function, please read on. In the prior chapter, I stated that we all live in the Milky Way Galaxy. It is our home, but the Milky Way Galaxy is only one simple spiral galaxy from among hundreds of billions of other galaxies in the known visible universe. Recently, the Hubble Telescope focused on a very small portion of the sky. This tiny little part of the sky was approximately the size of a pin hole (if you were to hold a needle and thread sized pin at approximately arms length). Within this tiny little pin hole section of the sky, the Hubble telescope took a 100 million second long exposure and uncovered hundreds of galaxies located at the very edge of our known universe. This can certainly seem mind boggling since this deep space exposure—from one seemingly insignificant, presumably empty, pinhole location of the sky—shows hundreds of galaxies with hundreds of millions of stars (at least) in each respective galaxy.

Astronomers are also finding that planets around stars are quite common. Currently, we can only observe the effects of these planets on the stars within our galaxy (because of the tremendous distances involved), but there is no reason to believe that other galaxies behave any differently than our own. After all, *Quantum Mechanics* and *General Relativity* basically operate the same way in almost all applicable situations, theoretically and in reality, except in instances such as black holes (although physicists have speculated that *String Theory* may answer all questions related to the universe in one unified theory). As a brief side note, black holes are simply super massive stars that have "burned up" (fused) all of their hydrogen and have reached the end of their lives. Some ordinary stars shed their outer layers of gas in a nonexplosive fashion and become planetary nebulas. Other stars simply dwindle down into white dwarfs. Some dying stars, however, catapult most of their mass into space as they gravitationally collapse in on themselves and explode as novas or supernovas. These exploding stars can ultimately become highly dense neutron stars and pulsars as they gravitationally collapse in on themselves, or they can become black holes. For the latter, depending on the mass of the star, gravity can sometimes become so great that light cannot escape the dying star's gravity. A black hole, therefore, is not really a hole. It's a super dense area of space that you just can't see because its tremendous gravity pulls everything into it. Even light can't escape.

That being said, every atom, molecule, and heavy element in our bodies was created somewhere during the collapse and explosion of a dying star (whether it becomes a black hole or not). This is generally the end result of hydrogen and helium fusion in a massive star. Therefore, any and all of the heavier elements in a Chemist's Periodic Table, including iron, carbon, copper, magnesium, calcium, potassium, and zinc (simply look at a vitamin/mineral supplement label) can only be formed through the nuclear fusion that occurs within a star. These heavier elements are then catapulted into space during a nova or supernova explosion. The age old alchemists who attempted in vain to convert worthless elements into gold were technically correct, but they never realized that they needed a giant fusion furnace—such as a dying star during a supernova—to create and then emancipate these heavier elements. According to modern Astronomers, the nuclear fusion that occurs within our own star, the Sun, releases gamma radiation that is equivalent to the energy that would be released from the explosion of 100 billion one-megaton hydrogen bombs per second. The ancient Alchemists, of course, simply didn't have such a device at their disposal.

Eventually these supernova created heavier elements are gravitationally brought together with hydrogen over millions of years of hurtling through space, and if enough hydrogen gas coalesces into another dense massive orb of gas, the pressure exerted on its gaseous core will ignite a nuclear reaction and create a new star. The heavier elements may then develop into planets, moons, and asteroids—and eventually, they might even become part of something living, like ourselves. That's basically how our Sun and solar system was formed. Then the cycle begins all over again. As a matter of fact, if Jupiter had been a much larger ball of hydrogen gas (Jupiter has no solid surface), the pressure exerted upon its core would have increased Jupiter's internal temperature so as to trigger a nuclear reaction. Our Earth would then have existed in a two star solar system. Both the Sun and Jupiter would have been stars.

In any case, there are so many stars in this enormous universe of ours that the potential for life in the cosmos is far greater than we had ever realized. As a matter of fact, Astronomers have clearly discovered that life exists on a *Class M* planet located in the Milky Way Galaxy. Even though the galaxy has between 200 billion and 400 billion stars, the life bearing planet is ideally situated within a solitary *Class G* star system that is orbiting at approximately 26,000 lights years from the center of the galaxy. This is a concrete fact. There is absolutely no question or doubt about it. Scientists have enormous amounts of proof. Quite simply, the *Class G* star is our Sun, and the *Class M* planet with life is Earth.

This is enormously significant. The fact that life has developed anywhere at all in the cosmos is extremely suggestive. It suggests that life can actually originate and arise **somewhere** in the universe. Furthermore, there are simply too many stars in the cosmos—billions of galaxies with hundreds of millions to hundreds of billions of stars per galaxy—for life to evolve on one planet alone. Mathematically and statistically speaking, the odds are phenomenally good that life also exists elsewhere. It even seems somewhat unfathomable that a universe so massive in size (with light taking 10–15 billion years to reach us from the very edge of our known universe) would allow the Earth to become so statistically unique in the overall scheme of things that life could only evolve here.

So what has all this got to do with Jesus? Well, we are simply all living hydrogen fusion gas byproducts of a violent and turbulent universe. We are subject to the same Laws of Physics that stars, planets, galaxies, and maybe even some black holes are subject to. If you also believe that God created a universe that is regulated by certain Laws of Physics, then perhaps God also created a set of physical laws that regulate the molecular energy and individual actions of all living things. If every molecule in our bodies is the result of some collapsing star's fusion process elsewhere in the universe—operating under the Laws of Physics—then is it so presumptuous to think that our actions might produce a physical cause and effect energy that ultimately returns to us in one shape, form, or another? Wouldn't that be real justice? People would never get away with murder, literally, and no one would be able to inflict atrocities on another without some penalty being imposed or without having the negative energy eventually return.

Some call this law Karma. I know this term has that Far Eastern "what's that got to do with us" sound to it, and I'm not going to try to prove or discredit this theory or belief. Let's just assume for argument sake that it is true. I am paraphrasing to some extent, but let's also assume *"that as you sow, so shall you reap"* and *"do unto others as you would have them do unto you"* are phrases that tie in with what some call Karma. You may even hear some say *"what goes around, comes around."*

Some people will even say that Karma requires us to return lifetime after lifetime to work out these karmic energies. For Kabbalists, this concept is called Tikun. Whether you call it Karma or Tikun—or whatever name you like—this energy is simply the cause and effect baggage that we initially take into this life from other lives. If you don't believe in Reincarnation, that's all right. Reincarnation is also not an easily proven philosophy or theory, but let's use a little bit of logic here. If you believe there is a God (a universal energy or divine consciousness) then logic would dictate that there must be some kind of system in the universe. The science of Physics certainly points out that the universe is ruled by certain physical laws, and that our universe might in some respects be a cause and effect mechanical universe that is explained in one form or another by physicists' theories such as *Quantum Mechanics*, Einstein's *Theory of Relativity*, and *String Theory*.

Karma and Reincarnation, however, may also adequately explain cause and effect energies and injustice in the world. Both these concepts clarify why some people are born into negative situations while others are born with seemingly exceptional opportunities. By living only once, God's universe doesn't seem fair, but if we reincarnate over and over, everything begins to make sense. Unfortunately, nothing will make any sense if you believe that the universe is just random chaos. Nevertheless, everyone does seem to have different lessons to learn while on this planet. If everyone only lived one life, wouldn't God have us all learn the same lesson? Wouldn't that be fair? Wouldn't that make sense?

There are some, however, who will say that there is no God or that God is not fair and his justice is not equally and fairly dispensed. But what if it is? Certainly the concepts of Heaven and Hell try to explain the handling of God's justice, but Reincarnation stipulates that cause and effect energies also allow God's justice to be dispensed since it causes one to experience the return of karmic energy, sin, or one's Tikun from one experience to the next, and if necessary, from one lifetime to the next. For example, if someone murdered another person in a previous lifetime—and seemed to get away with it—then the individual could now be falsely accused of murder and be convicted of something that he or she did not commit in this lifetime. Or perhaps the person might have to experience the karmic energy of actually being murdered. Or perhaps the individual might have to live through the anguish of having someone close to them murdered. Don't hold me to this. I can't say exactly how the universe (God) handles these types of situations, but this basically is the essence of Reincarnation and Karma according to Buddhism, Hinduism, those who study Kabbalah, as well as other schools of religious and philosophical thought. Even old fashioned Orthodox Fundamentalist

Jews believe in Reincarnation. According to the Jewish historian, Josephus, the Pharisees and the Essenes of Jesus' time also believed in Reincarnation.

Once again, I am not trying to promote Karma and Reincarnation as 100% fact. Whether we live once or a thousand times is basically not relevant since the only life that really counts is the one we are living right now. It's really quite simple. If Karma and Reincarnation really do exist, **what better way for us to learn than to have us experience the same karmic, sinning, or Tikun energy that we caused another to experience?** If we hate others, then we need to feel hate directed toward us. If we steal from another, then we must experience what it's like to be stolen from. If we judge others, then we have to find out what it's like to be judged. If we lie to others, then we will need to experience others lying to us. In short, the world is a "**Mirror.**" These energies are simply a reflection of our own energies. Those things in the world and in others that we don't like or approve of, exist in one form or another within us (whether they are active or dormant; from this lifetime or a previous one). The primary reason they disturb or annoy us is that there is a karmic or Tikun lesson that needs to be learned, resolved, or corrected that is associated with the energy we are reacting to. **It seems to be one of the most logical ways for God to have us understand the sin or karmic energy that we have dealt to another.** In some ways, it's the only thing that makes sense in a universe that, in all other respects, appears to function and operate according to various physical laws. Once again, if God did "create" scientific laws to ensure the proper maintenance of this enormous mechanical universe—a giant cosmic machine if you will—then why would God not create a set of rules that relate to the "soul" of an individual? If the soul is a form of consciousness or energy, then why not have that energy keep returning to learn from its mistakes? This strikes me as a more merciful and useful way for someone to grow and evolve rather than being sent to Hell for eternity with no hope of finding one's way back to God. Is one life really enough to learn how things work? Is one life really enough for a soul to find its way back to God?

Reincarnation may actually be similar in analogy to a child graduating from one grade to the next. There's always more to learn. Sometimes you even get "left back" and have to do the grade again. Other times you move onto the next grade for new lessons. Hopefully, we get to graduate after many lives and move onto something else. Whatever that might be.

As mentioned, Christianity created a Heaven and a Hell to sort these things out. Are Karma and Reincarnation any more farfetched than these concepts? Everyone has varying forms of intelligence, different levels of experience, and contrasting skills to deal with the problems that beset all mankind. Isn't it easier for a rich man not to steal, than a poor man who has nothing? While the rich man may perhaps have a karmic lesson related to power and the possible abuse of it, the poor man may have a karmic lesson related to resentment, that things are not fair, so "…why play by the rules." The poor man may even think that the rules are set up by those who have vs. those who have not. This is just an arbitrary example. Theoretically, in the next life the roles for these two people may actually be reversed if the lessons are not correctly learned. For example, if the rich man made a considerable effort in using his power to ostracize or falsely accuse the poor man of some crime—perhaps to obtain his property—then this rich man could return in another lifetime as a poor man and experience having someone falsely accuse him to obtain his property. Again, these are simply hypotheticals.

There is, however, a clear inherent danger with this type of philosophy or belief. Does everyone who experiences a terrible crime in this life have a negative experience simply because of prior negative karma or because of a Kabbalistic cause and effect Tikun? This belief can be an extremely dangerous one. A woman being raped, a serial killer choosing people at random, or any other senseless act of violence should not always be nonchalantly considered as the return of that victim's prior life karmic energy or sin. New karma can and does occur. In fact, wasn't there and didn't there have to be a first sin or negative karmic energy at some point in time?

Furthermore, if life does exist on other planets in this universe, does God also need to have Jesus crucified, sacrificed, and murdered to save these other worlds? Are some of these planets still living in perfection because they didn't sin in their own particular Gardens of Eden? If you really think about it, God needing to sacrifice his own son for humanity is such an ancient, brutal, and even bizarre concept that one cannot help but wonder how modern people could still believe such an archaic belief. In short, did God really require a human sacrifice and have his own son murdered to save us from our sins? Furthermore, does the belief in this brutal human sacrifice subsequently allow us entry into Heaven if we truly believe that Jesus died for our sins?

In any case, there must be one rule **THAT WE MUST ALWAYS FOLLOW**. Never be the first to sin or cause karma to another. This may incur a debt that will have to be repaid. If someone causes a karmic act or sins against us, we must choose "…to turn the other cheek…" as Jesus suggested in Matthew 5:39. Jesus made this statement because he understood that there was a karmic energy associated with feelings of anger or hatred or even the desire for revenge itself. If we are sinned against, one must try to leave it in God's hands. Mankind's laws will handle many karmic energies and crimes. When mankind's laws don't seem to work, and when justice seems like injustice, perhaps a karmic debt does become associated with an individual who purposely inflicts a negative experience onto another.

God may also give everyone the opportunity to be honestly remorseful for their karmic or sinful act. For lack of a better term, we may be allowed to "repent" our karmic actions or sins. If we are truly sorry for our negative actions, this may possibly temper and soften the severity of the negative karmic energies when they do return. In short, the universe (God) may allow a type of temperance or clemency of the returning karmic energy in direct proportion to the severity of the lesson needed. An unlearned lesson may require a more harsh retribution. A learned lesson may not require Karma to be as severe. A learned lesson may also eradicate the need for any returning negative energy at all. In essence, isn't this what Jesus might have been trying to teach us almost 2,000 years ago? Once again Jesus' message was very simple.

(1) Love God with all your heart, soul, and mind.

(2) Do to others only what you would have them do to you.

(3) Don't judge others or you'll risk judgement upon yourself.

(4) Love your neighbor as yourself.

Lastly, suffering usually prompts some type of understanding and learning. When suffering does not prompt a learning experience, it is because we are oblivious to the karmic issue or the Tikun that we need to deal with. If the cause and effect concepts of Karma and Tikun are accurate, then our discomfort and suffering should begin to dissipate once we understand why we are experiencing the associated pain. We will then experience a temporary lull before the next life lesson begins to exert itself. Life is a series of these lessons, one after another, with death being "the vacation" between one life and the next.

Is this how life may actually work? These concepts are common themes in many religions and belief structures such as Buddhism, Hinduism, and those who study Kabbalah. As of late, Kabbalah is growing in popularity within the United States. Concepts of Buddhism have been more readily accepted as well. These two particular belief systems are very much aware of the principle of cause and effect.

In contrast, where Chinese/Tibetan Buddhism states that you should always strive for detachment from (negative) feelings and energies, those who practice

Kabbalah embrace conflict and negative energies as a means to grow and learn. Both also state that we feel pain because we have allowed circumstances and other individuals to affect us. If we ultimately learn what is causing the negative energy to arise, we are "absolved" of the energy causing us pain. This occurs because we've learned the lesson associated with it. Furthermore, if we acknowledge that we are creating new outbound negative karmic energy, and if we also diligently attempt to stop this "sinning toward another," then the karmic pain associated with this action will also diminish. Pain is simply God's way of saying that we are off-balance, off-centered, and living with or exerting negative karmic or sinful energies.

In closing, Jesus would certainly be mortified at how many people have been killed in his name. He would also be disappointed at the judgements that people still project onto others today. Jesus might also be deeply saddened that his message had been changed and modified so dramatically—and that he was ultimately turned into a deity by Christians who perhaps meant well, but had unfortunately misinterpreted his original and true message of love.

It appears that Christians have almost always misunderstood why Jesus was here. He did not come to "save us" as the New Testament books of John and Paul would have us believe. It was to show us a way back to God. Jesus provided us with an example. He also showed us that we could talk directly to God without the need of intervention from a priest, rabbi, minister, monk, or other miscellaneous cleric. According to the New Testament, Jesus also tried to show that there was a life beyond this one, otherwise why be resurrected from the dead, appear to his disciples, and show them that life does exist beyond death? Jesus also seems to have set such an extraordinary example of wisdom and enlightenment, throughout his last years of life, that he should certainly be worthy of our respect, our reverence, and maybe even our awe.

It's also extraordinary that Jesus' basic underlying message still exists today, considering how much has been changed by those who had never met or heard Jesus speak. If you also take the time to look at Jesus's words only, you will get a much clearer and distinct idea of what he really said. In fact, the next time you really want to know what Jesus may have taught, just sit down and **only** read the New Testament books of Matthew, Mark, and Luke. Finally, always try to remember that the New Testament that exists today is the result of various miscellaneous decisions made during the fourth century where many Christian texts were simply eliminated and ignored by church authorities. At the risk of being redundant, it would also be wise to give a certain amount of serious skepticism to those books ascribed to the Apostle Paul and the Disciple John. As mentioned earlier, Jesus uses an analogy that you can ascertain the quality of a religion or a prophet by the fruit it provides (Matthew 7:16-20 and Matthew 12:33). If a prophet or a religion bears bad fruit, it cannot be recommended as a good source. If the fruit is bad, the source is probably bad. Quite simply, Jesus' teachings had been misunderstood and distorted, and Paul and John are prophets that have inadvertently produced a good deal of bad fruit.

We can also indulge in questioning whether Jesus was the Christ, an anointed messenger from God, a prophet, a Jewish Kabbalistic Mystic, a Bodhisattva (an advanced soul with a special purpose to help humanity), the Son of God, or even God himself as part of the Trinity, but is there a direct logical solution or answer to this question? Perhaps not. Nonetheless, Jesus is highly respected, venerated, and revered in many religions. He is a major prophet in the Muslim's Holy Koran. He is accepted as an incarnation of love in Buddhism. The Jews even recognize Jesus, at the very least, as the founder of Christianity. Furthermore, it does seem that every now and then, an advanced soul, a Bodhisattva, or just a plain old visionary seems to descend to Earth, and man in his infinite wisdom manages to somehow misunderstand, distort, or change the message. Or even worse, with human nature sometimes being what it is, man will feel compelled to ridicule, manipulate, oppress, or persecute this human being in an attempt to change, hinder, control, or even destroy the individual's message.

End

Selected Bibliography

Alighieri, Dante. *The Inferno*. New York: Mentor Books, 1954.

Augustine, Saint. *Confessions*. Baltimore: Penguin Books, 1969.

Benware, P.N. *Survey of the New Testament*. Chicago: Moody Press, 1990.

Berg, Yehuda. *The Power of Kabbalah, Technology for the Soul*. New York: The Kabbalah Centre, 2004

Berg, Yehuda. *The 72 Names of God*. New York: The Kabbalah Centre, 2003.

Bettenson, Henry. *Documents of the Christian Church*. New York: Oxford University Press, 1947.

Brundage, James A. *Law, Sex, and Christian Society in Medieval Europe*. Chicago: The University of Chicago Press, 1987.

Cohen, A. *The Psalms, A Translation*. London: The Soncino Press, 1958.

Collins, Raymond F. *Introduction to the New Testament*. Garden City: Doubleday and Company, 1983.

Dalpadado, J. Kingsley. *Reading the Gospels*. Boston: The Daughters of St. Paul, 1981.

Farmer, William R. *Jesus and the Gospels*. Philadelphia: Fortress Press, 1982.

Finegan, Jack. *Handbook of Biblical Chronology*. Princeton: Princeton University Press, 1964.

Fitzmeyer, Joseph A. *The Anchor Bible*. Garden City: Doubleday and Company, 1985.

Greene, Brian. *The Elegant Universe: Superstrings, Hidden Dimensions, and the Quest for the Ultimate Theory*. New York: Vintage Books, 2000.

Hawkings, Stephen. *A Brief History of Time: The Updated and Expanded Tenth Anniversary Edition*. New York: Bantam, 1998.

Hsing, Chang. *The Teachings of the Buddha*. Translated by Lok To. Edited by Frank French. New York: Young Men's Buddhist Association of America, 2001.

Holcomb, Katherine A., and John Frederick Hawley. *Foundations of Modern Cosmology*. New York: Oxford University Press, 1998.

Holy Bible, Revised Standard Version. New York: Thomas Nelson and Sons, 1953.

Holy Bible, New King James Version. New York: Thomas Nelson Publishers, 1982.

Josephus, Flavius. *Josephus, Complete Works*. Grand Rapids: Kregel Publications, 1960.

Karras, Ruth Mazo. *Common Women: Prostitution and Sexuality in Medieval England (Studies in the History of Sexuality)*. New York: Oxford University Press, 1996.

Lahaye, Tim, and Jerry B. Jenkins. *Left Behind, A Novel of the Earth's Last Days*. Wheaton: Tyndale House Publishers, 1995.

Laymon, C.M. *The Interpreter's One Volume Commentary on the Bible*. Nashville: Abingdon Press, 1991.

Layton, Bentley. *The Gnostic Scriptures (A Translation)*. Garden City: Doubleday and Company, 1987.

McDowell, Josh. *Evidence that Demands a Verdict*. San Bernardino: Here's Life Publishers, 1979.

Meyer, Marvin. *The Gospels of Mary*. San Francisco: Harpers San Francisco, 2004.

Netanyahu, B. *The Origins of the Inquisition in Fifteenth Century Spain*. New York: New York Review of Books, 2001.

New Testament of the Jerusalem Bible. Garden City: Doubleday and Company, 1969.

New Encyclopedia Britannica. London: 15th Edition, Volume 22, 1974.

Page, Susan. "Churchgoing Closely Tied to Voting Patterns," *USA Today*, 2 June 2004.

Plummer, Alfred. *The International Critical Commentary*. New York: Charles Schribner's Sons, 1960.

Rahula, Walpola. *What the Buddha Taught*. New York: Grove Press, 1956.

Richards, Jeffrey. *Dissidence and Damnation: Minority Groups in the Middle Ages*. New York: Routledge, 1994.

Robinson, James M. *The Nag Hammadi Library*. San Francisco: Harper and Row, Publishers, 1977.

Santini, Peter Della. *The Tree of Enlightenment, An Introduction to the Major Traditions of Buddhism*. Taipei: Chico Dharma Study Foundation, 1997.

Santini, Peter D. *Fundamentals of Buddhism*. Carmel: The Institute for Advanced Studies of World Religions, Chuang Yen Monastery, 2001.

Schonfield, Hugh J. *The Passover Plot*. New York: Bernard Geis Associates/Random House, 1965.

Slotki, I.W. *Isaiah, A Translation*. London: The Soncino Press, 1959.

Tatum, W. Barnes. *In Quest of Jesus*. Atlanta: John Knox Press, 1982.

Unger, Merrill F. *Unger's Bible Dictionary*. Chicago: Moody Press, 1966.

Vermes, Geza. *The Dead Sea Scrolls*. New York: Heritage Press, 1967.

Willmington, H.R. *Bible Handbook*. Wheaton: Tyndale House Publishers, 1997.

Wilson, A.N. *Paul, The Mind of the Apostle*. New York: W.W. Norton and Company, 1997.

Zombeck, Martin V. *Handbook of Space Astronomy and Astrophysics*. Cambridge: Cambridge University Press, 1990.

To Contact The Author

PeterCayce@aol.com
P.O. Box 293
Stormville, New York 12582

(Due To Computer Virus And Firewall Security Issues, Not All Emails May Be Read)

0-595-32673-0

Printed in the United Kingdom
by Lightning Source UK Ltd.
117711UKS00001B/347